The
Nativity

The Nativity

Alonzo L. Gaskill

DESERET BOOK

SALT LAKE CITY, UTAH

DESERET BOOK is a registered trademark of Deseret Book Company.

Visit us at DeseretBook.com

Library of Congress Cataloging-in-Publication Data

Gaskill, Alonzo L.
 The nativity / Alonzo L. Gaskill.
  p. cm.
 Includes bibliographical references and index.
 ISBN-10 1-59038-527-6 (pbk.)
 ISBN-13 978-1-59038-527-2 (pbk.)
 1. Jesus Christ—Nativity. 2. Jesus Christ—Mormon interpretations.
I. Title.
BX8643.J4G37 2006
232.92—dc22   2006014456

Printed in the United States of America
Alexander's Print Advantage, Lindon, UT

JIT

To my parents
Diana and Gary Gaskill
who instilled in me from my youth
a deep love for the holidays

CONTENTS

CONTENTS

PREFACE

The practice of reading the story of the Nativity as part of annual Christmas celebrations is such a popular and powerful tradition among Latter-day Saints that a detailed look seems appropriate. Of course, the Christmas story proper consists of only four chapters in the New Testament—in fact, just four of a total of eighty-nine chapters in the Gospels. Nonetheless, the importance of the words contained in those four chapters far outweighs their length. The tangible and pervasive spirit that is felt at Christmastime is undeniable and certainly warrants our attention.

An added motivation for this book comes from my experience in teaching the first two chapters of Matthew and Luke. In years past I gave a Christmas quiz of sorts to my students. Invariably, most would score rather poorly, confusing many of the standard elements of the story and often manifesting a better knowledge of popular cultural interpretations than of the actual teachings of scripture. If for no other reason than this, a close look at the story of Christ's birth would be beneficial. Indeed, as so many of the particulars of the Christmas story tend to be confused, the reader is encouraged to take the Christmas Quiz (Appendix 1) *before* reading the remainder of this book.

In addition to the writings of Latter-day Saints, this book draws from ancient and modern non–Latter-day Saint religious texts. Of course, these do not formulate doctrine. That comes *only* from the Lord through His authorized servants—the divinely called and appointed prophets and apostles. However, as is borne out by Latter-day Saints' fascination with C. S. Lewis, some non-LDS sources seem to see the gospel through lenses very similar to our own. Where an early Church Father or a contemporary non-LDS theologian offers insights or applications of a verse that seem harmonious with the position of the Church, I have felt comfortable quoting them.[1]

Finally, my focus in writing this small work has been for members of the Church rather than biblical scholars. Its primary purpose is to enable those who read the New Testament Christmas story each year to do so with a better understanding of those sacred and foreordained events.

ACKNOWLEDGMENTS

I offer my sincere appreciation to the following individuals: Cory Maxwell, of Deseret Book, who saw value in this manuscript and worked to bring it into print; Dr. Gaye Strathearn, of Brigham Young University, for her thorough review of the text and helpful suggestions; and Dr. Richard Draper, also of Brigham Young University, who encouraged me while in his humble way pointing out pitfalls.

CHAPTER ONE

A HARMONY OF MATTHEW'S AND LUKE'S ACCOUNTS OF THE BIRTH OF CHRIST

Neither of the two biblical accounts of Christ's nativity contains all of the details traditionally recited or read each Christmas by faithful Christians throughout the world. In fact, Matthew and Luke seem almost evenly divided on what details they do provide, and there is minimal crossover in their content, with the sole exception of their primary focus—the divine birth and messianic calling of the Lord Jesus Christ. Concerning why Matthew and Luke cover such vastly different elements, while leaving out others, one eighth-century Church Father wrote:

> Individual Evangelists are prone to omit certain things, which they see were recorded by others, or which they foresee in the Spirit will be recorded by others, so that in the continuous thread of their narration nothing seems omitted. What has thus been passed over [in one Gospel], the diligent reader will

discover by carefully going through each of the Gospels in turn.[1]

Such has been borne out in the Book of Mormon, for when Nephi saw the vision that was later to be received by John the Revelator, he was forbidden by the Lord to write it, for John was to be given the divine calling to record those sacred truths that he and others had been permitted to see (1 Nephi 14:18–28). Similarly, one Latter-day Saint commentator noted:

> The sum of the parts becomes greater than the whole; that is, . . . in their union comes an understanding that cannot otherwise be had. This is simply an expression of the law of witnesses. . . . Not only do the separate witnesses corroborate each other but they also expand, extend, and enhance each other. So it is that the testimonies relative to the birth of Christ . . . join together to fortify and enrich our understanding of the doctrine of the divine sonship of Christ.[2]

The following harmony gathers into one ordered text all that Matthew and Luke recorded about the nativity of Christ. Words in *italics* represent changes to the King

James Version of the text from the Joseph Smith Translation of the Bible.[3]

Luke 1:26	And in the sixth month [of Elisabeth's pregnancy] the angel Gabriel was sent from God unto a city of Galilee, named Nazareth,
Luke 1:27	To a virgin espoused to a man whose name was Joseph, of the house of David; and the virgin's name was Mary.
Luke 1:28	And the angel came in unto her and said, Hail, *thou virgin, who art highly favored of the Lord. The Lord is with thee, for thou art chosen and blessed among women.*
Luke 1:29	And when she saw *the angel,* she was troubled at his saying, and *pondered* in her mind what manner of salutation this should be.
Luke 1:30	And the angel said unto her, Fear not, Mary: for thou hast found favour with God.
Luke 1:31	And, behold, thou shalt conceive,[4] and bring forth a son, and *shall* call his name Jesus.

Luke 1:32   He shall be great, and shall be called the Son of the Highest: and the Lord God shall give unto him the throne of his father David:

Luke 1:33   And he shall reign over the house of Jacob for ever; and of his kingdom there shall be no end.

Luke 1:34   Then said Mary unto the angel, *How can this be?*[5]

Luke 1:35   And the angel answered and said unto her, *Of the Holy Ghost, and the power of the Highest. Therefore also, that holy child that* shall be born of thee shall be called the Son of God.

Luke 1:36   And, behold, thy cousin Elisabeth, she hath also conceived a son in her old age; and this is the sixth month with her, who *is* called barren.

Luke 1:37   For with God nothing *can* be impossible.

Luke 1:38   And Mary said, Behold the handmaid of the Lord; be it unto me according to thy word. And the angel departed from her.

Luke 1:39	*And in those days, Mary* went into the hill country with haste, into a city of Juda,
Luke 1:40	And entered into the house of Zacharias, and saluted Elisabeth.
Luke 1:41	And it came to pass, that, when Elisabeth heard the salutation of Mary, the babe leaped in her womb; and Elisabeth was filled with the Holy Ghost:
Luke 1:42	And she spake out with a loud voice, and said, Blessed art thou among women, and blessed is the fruit of thy womb.
Luke 1:43	*And why is it, that this blessing is upon me,* that the mother of my Lord should come to me?
Luke 1:44	For, lo, as soon as the voice of thy salutation sounded in mine ears, the babe leaped in my womb for joy.
Luke 1:45	And blessed *art thou who* believed: *for those things which were told thee by the angel of the Lord, shall be fulfilled.*
Luke 1:46	And Mary said, My soul doth magnify the Lord,
Luke 1:47	And my spirit *rejoiceth* in God my Saviour.

Luke 1:48   For he hath regarded the low estate of his handmaiden: for, behold, from henceforth all generations shall call me blessed.

Luke 1:49   For he *who is* mighty hath done to me great things; *and I will magnify his holy name,*

Luke 1:50   *For* his mercy is *on those who* fear him from generation to generation.

Luke 1:51   He hath shewed strength with his arm; he hath scattered the proud in the imagination of their hearts.

Luke 1:52   He hath put down the mighty from their seats, and exalted them of low degree.

Luke 1:53   He hath filled the hungry with good things; *but* the rich he hath sent empty away.

Luke 1:54   He hath *helped* his servant Israel in remembrance of his mercy,

Luke 1:55   As he spake to our fathers, to Abraham, and to his seed for ever.

Luke 1:56   And Mary abode with *Elisabeth* about three months, and returned to her own house.

Matthew 1:18 Now, *as it is written,* the birth of Jesus Christ was on this wise. *After* his mother, Mary, was espoused to Joseph, before they came together, she was found with child of the Holy Ghost.

Matthew 1:19 Then Joseph her husband, being a just man, and not willing to make her a publick example, was minded to put her away privily.

Matthew 1:20 But while he thought on these things, behold, the angel of the Lord appeared unto him in a *vision,* saying, Joseph, thou son of David, fear not to take unto thee Mary thy wife; for that which is conceived in her, is of the Holy Ghost.

Matthew 1:21 And she shall bring forth a son, and thou shalt call his name JESUS: for he shall save his people from their sins.

Matthew 1:22 *Now this took place, that all things* might be fulfilled, which *were* spoken of the Lord, by the *prophets,* saying,

Matthew 1:23 Behold, a virgin shall be with child, and shall bring forth a son, and they shall call

his name Emmanuel, which being interpreted is, God with us.

Matthew 1:24   Then Joseph, *awaking out of his vision,*
did as the angel of the Lord had bidden
him, and took unto him his wife;

Luke 2:1   And it came to pass in those days, that
there went out a decree from Caesar
Augustus, that all *his empire* should be
taxed.

Luke 2:2   *This same taxing was when Cyrenius was
governor of Syria.*

Luke 2:3   And all went to be taxed, every one *in* his
own city.

Luke 2:4   And Joseph also went up from Galilee,
out of the city of Nazareth, into Judaea,
unto the city of David, which is called
Bethlehem; (because he was of the house
and lineage of David:)

Luke 2:5   To be taxed, with Mary his espoused
wife, *she* being great with child.

Matthew 1:25a   And [Joseph] knew her not till she had
brought forth her firstborn son:

Luke 2:6   And so it was, that, while they were there,

the days were accomplished that she should be delivered.

Luke 2:7   And she brought forth her firstborn son, and wrapped him in swaddling clothes, and laid him in a manger; because there was *none to give room for them in the inns.*

Matthew 1:25b . . . and *they* called his name JESUS.

Luke 2:8   And there were in the same country, shepherds abiding in the field, keeping watch over their *flocks* by night.

Luke 2:9   And lo, *an* angel of the Lord *appeared unto* them, and the glory of the Lord shone round about them; and they were sore afraid.

Luke 2:10   *But* the angel said unto them, Fear not, for behold, I bring you good tidings of great joy, which shall be to all people.

Luke 2:11   For unto you is born this day, in the city of David, a *Savior, who* is Christ the Lord.

Luke 2:12   And this *is the way you shall find the babe, he is* wrapped in swaddling clothes, *and is* lying in a manger.

Luke 2:13   And suddenly there was with the angel a

multitude of the heavenly host praising God, and saying,

Luke 2:14   Glory to God in the highest; and on earth, peace; goodwill *to* men.

Luke 2:15   And it came to pass, *when* the angels were gone away from them into heaven, the shepherds said one to another, Let us now go, even unto Bethlehem, and see this thing which is come to pass, which the Lord *has* made known unto us.

Luke 2:16   And they came with haste, and found Mary, and Joseph, and the babe lying in a manger.

Luke 2:17   And when they had seen,[6] they made known abroad the saying which was told them concerning this child.

Luke 2:18   *All they who heard it,* wondered at those things which were told them by the shepherds.

Luke 2:19   But Mary kept all these things, and pondered them in her heart.

Luke 2:20   And the shepherds returned, glorifying and praising God for all the things *which* they had heard and seen, as *they were manifested unto them.*

Luke 2:21 And when eight days were accomplished for the circumcising of the child, his name was called JESUS; which was so named of the angel before he was conceived.[7]

Luke 2:22 And when the days of her purification according to the law of Moses were accomplished, they brought him to Jerusalem, to present him to the Lord;

Luke 2:23 As it is written in the law of the Lord, Every male *which* openeth the womb shall be called holy to the Lord;[8]

Luke 2:24 And to offer a sacrifice according to that which is *written* in the law of the Lord, A pair of turtledoves, or two young pigeons.

Luke 2:25 And behold, there was a man *at* Jerusalem, whose name was Simeon; and the same man was just and devout, waiting for the consolation of Israel; and the Holy Ghost was upon him.

Luke 2:26 And it was revealed unto him by the Holy

Ghost, that he should not see death, before he had seen the Lord's Christ.

Luke 2:27 And he came by the Spirit into the temple: and when the parents brought in the child, *even* Jesus, to do for him after the custom of the law,

Luke 2:28 Then took he him up in his arms, and blessed God, and said,

Luke 2:29 Lord, now lettest[9] thy servant depart in peace, according to thy word;

Luke 2:30 For mine eyes have seen thy salvation,

Luke 2:31 Which thou hast prepared before the face of all people;

Luke 2:32 A light to lighten the Gentiles, and the glory of thy people Israel.

Luke 2:33 And Joseph, and[10] *Mary,* marvelled at those things which were spoken of *the child.*

Luke 2:34 And Simeon blessed them, and said unto Mary,[11] Behold, this child is set for the fall and rising again of many in Israel; and for a sign which shall be spoken against;

Luke 2:35 Yea, a *spear* shall pierce through *him to*

the wounding of thine own soul also;[12] that the thoughts of many hearts may be revealed.

Luke 2:36   And there was one Anna, a prophetess, the daughter of Phanuel, of the tribe of *Asher.* She was of a great age, and had lived with *a* husband *only* seven years, *whom she married in her youth,*

Luke 2:37   And she *lived* a widow of about fourscore and four years, *who* departed not from the temple, but served God with fastings and prayers, night and day.

Luke 2:38   And she, coming in that instant, gave thanks likewise unto the Lord, and spake of him, to all *those who* looked for redemption in Jerusalem.[13]

Matthew 2:1 Now when Jesus was born in Bethlehem of Judaea in the days of Herod the king, behold, there came wise men from the east to Jerusalem,

Matthew 2:2 Saying, Where is *the child* that is born, *the Messiah* of the Jews? for we have seen his star in the east, and are come to worship him.

Matthew 2:3   When Herod the king had heard *of the child,* he was troubled, and all Jerusalem with him.

Matthew 2:4   And when he had gathered all the chief priests, and scribes of the people together, he demanded of them, *saying, Where is the place that is written of by the prophets, in which* Christ should be born? *For he greatly feared, yet he believed not the prophets.*

Matthew 2:5   And they said unto him, *It is written by the prophets, that he should be born* in Bethlehem of Judaea, *for thus have they said,*

Matthew 2:6   *The word of the Lord came unto us, saying,* And thou Bethlehem, *which lieth* in the land of *Judea, in thee shall be born a prince, which* art not the least among the princes of *Judea;* for out of thee shall come *the Messiah, who* shall *save* my people Israel.

Matthew 2:7   Then Herod, when he had *called the wise men privily, inquired* of them diligently what time the star appeared.

Matthew 2:8   And he sent them to Bethlehem, and said, Go and search diligently for the young child; and when ye have found *the child,* bring me word again, that I may come and worship him also.

Matthew 2:9 When they had heard the king, they departed; and lo, the star which they saw in the east, went before them, *until* it came and stood over where the young child was.

Matthew 2:10 When they saw the star, they rejoiced with exceeding great joy.

Matthew 2:11 And when they were come into the house, they saw the young child with Mary his mother, and fell down, and worshipped him: and when they had opened their treasures, they presented unto him gifts; gold, and frankincense, and myrrh.

Matthew 2:12 And being warned of God in a dream that they should not return to Herod, they departed into their own country another way.

Matthew 2:13 And when they were departed, behold, the angel of the Lord *appeared* to Joseph in a *vision,* saying, Arise and take the young child and his mother, and flee into

Egypt, and *tarry* thou there until I bring thee word; for Herod will seek the young child to destroy him.

Matthew 2:14 *And then* he arose, *and* took the young child, and *the child's* mother, by night, and departed into Egypt;

Matthew 2:15 And was there until the death of Herod: that it might be fulfilled which was spoken of the Lord by the prophet, saying, Out of Egypt have I called my son.

Matthew 2:16 Then Herod, when he saw that he was mocked of the wise men, was exceeding wroth; and sent forth and slew all the children that were in Bethlehem, and in all the coasts thereof, from two years old and under, according to the time which he had diligently *inquired* of the wise men.

Matthew 2:17 Then was fulfilled that which was spoken by *Jeremiah* the prophet, saying,

Matthew 2:18 In *Ramah there* was a voice heard, lamentation, and weeping, and great mourning; *Rachael* weeping for *the loss of* her children, and would not be comforted because they *were* not.

Matthew 2:19 But when Herod was dead, behold, an angel of the Lord *appeared* in a *vision* to Joseph in Egypt,

Matthew 2:20 Saying, Arise, and take the young child and his mother, and go into the land of Israel; for they are dead *who* sought the young child's life.

Matthew 2:21 And he arose, and took the young child and his mother, and came into the land of Israel.

Matthew 2:22 But when he heard that Archelaus did reign in *Judea,* in the *stead* of his father Herod, he was afraid to go thither; *but* notwithstanding, being warned of God in a *vision,* he *went* into the *eastern part* of Galilee;

Matthew 2:23 And he came and dwelt in a city called Nazareth: that it might be fulfilled which was spoken by the prophets, He shall be called a Nazarene.

Luke 2:40 And the child grew, and waxed strong in spirit, *being* filled with wisdom, and the grace of God was upon him.

Chapter Two

Matthew's Account of the Birth of Christ

Through his Gospel account, Matthew bears witness of the divinity of the Lord Jesus Christ, offering his personal testimony as an apostle of the Lord Jesus Christ of the Savior's divine creation and heavenly origins.[1] Matthew's inspired work provides us with details regarding the Nativity of Christ which are found nowhere else in the New Testament.[2] What follows is a verse-by-verse examination of Matthew's account of Christ's birth as recorded in the King James Version of the Bible (in Matthew 1:18–2:22) and in the Joseph Smith Translation (in Matthew 2:1–3:26).

---•---

Matthew 1:18

Now the birth of Jesus Christ was on this wise: When as his mother Mary was espoused to

*Joseph, before they came together, she was
found with child of the Holy Ghost.*

Mary was espoused to Joseph

Espousal was akin to a legally binding marriage but
without the marital intimacy. The penalty for fornicating
with one who was espoused was death for both parties.
Indeed, so binding was a betrothal that should a young
girl's fiancé die before the marriage was consummated, she
would be considered a widow. Elder Bruce R. McConkie
wrote:

> Mary was espoused to Joseph, meaning she
> had made a formal contract of marriage with him
> that yet had to be completed in a second ceremony
> before they would commence living together as
> husband and wife. She was, however, considered by
> their law to be his wife; the contract could be bro-
> ken only by a formal "bill of divorcement," and
> any infidelity on her part would be classed as
> adultery.[3]

Similarly, biblical scholar Raymond E. Brown wrote:

> The Jewish Matrimonial procedure . . . con-
> sisted of two steps: a formal exchange of consent

before witnesses (Mal 2:14) and the subsequent taking of the bride to the groom's family home (Matt 25:1–13). While the term marriage is sometimes used to designate the second step, in terms of legal implications it would be more properly applied to the first step. The consent ("betrothal"), usually entered into when the girl was between twelve and thirteen years old, would constitute a legally ratified marriage in our terms, since it gave the young man rights over the girl. She was henceforth his wife (notice the term "wife," in Matt 1:20, 24), and any infringement on his marital rights could be punished as adultery. Yet the wife continued to live at her own family home, usually for about a year. Then took place the formal transferal or taking of the bride to the husband's family home where he assumed her support. . . . The wife had to be taken to her husband's home as a virgin. It is clear, explicitly in Matthew and implicitly in Luke (since Mary is betrothed but still a virgin) that Joseph and Mary are in the stage of matrimonial procedure between the two steps.[4]

Mary . . . was found with child of the Holy Ghost

Elder James E. Talmage suggested that Mary had been away at Elisabeth's for about three months before returning home. Upon her return, her size may have made it obvious to anyone who saw her that she was pregnant.[5] Similarly, the early Christian Protevangelium of James (a document attributed to James, the son of Joseph and Mary and thus half brother of Jesus) records: "And [Mary] was in her sixth month; and, behold, Joseph came . . . and, entering into his house, he discovered that she was big with child. And he . . . wept bitterly."[6] One can only imagine what was in the hearts of both Mary and Joseph at this heavily anticipated meeting.

Contrary to some popular Christian traditions, which take quite literally Matthew's statement that Mary's baby was "of the Holy Ghost," respected scholars acknowledge that Matthew's phrase "of the Holy Ghost" may give the false impression that Matthew is implying that the Holy Ghost is the father of Jesus. Yet such was never Matthew's intent.[7] The infant Christ is "the Son of God," not the son of the Holy Ghost. The scriptures and modern prophets have been quite clear on this point.[8] The Latter-day Saint position is that the text would be more accurately interpreted: Mary was with child by the *power* of the Holy Ghost. Nephi was instructed by the Spirit that God the Father would step down from His heavenly throne and beget His Only Begotten Son in the flesh (1 Nephi 11:18–20).[9]

President Joseph F. Smith put it this way:

> How are children begotten? I answer just as Jesus Christ was begotten of his father. The Christian denominations believe that Christ was begotten not of God but of the spirit that overshadowed his mother. This is nonsense. Why will not the world receive the truth? Why will they not believe the Father when he says that Jesus Christ is His only begotten Son? Why will they try to explain this truth away and make mystery of it?[10]

The importance of Jesus' parentage should not be ignored. He was, indeed, the Son of God and the son of mortal Mary. From His mother He received a mortal body; from His Divine Father He received the power both to surrender His life (it could not be taken from Him) and to take it up again. Without that power, there would have been no Atonement. And, of course, without the Atonement all of God's creations would be lost. Thus, the announcement in this verse (Matthew 1:18) that Jesus' parents were the mortal Mary and the Divine Father— even God—is not simply a passing side note. It is the primary point of the Nativity story and the central truth of the gospel plan. His unique birth would determine what He could do for fallen man. To a great extent, it is what we learn in the Nativity story that allows us to exercise faith in Christ and His innate ability to save us.

———————— • ————————

MATTHEW 1:19

Then Joseph her husband, being a just man,
and not willing to make her a publick example,
was minded to put her away privily.

Joseph . . . being a just man

The Greek word translated here as "just" can mean one who uses "righteous judgment"—"a man of character." Joseph's actions here establish that he was certainly that; however, the Greek can also mean that Joseph was "entirely obedient to the dictates of the Law," a law which required that an adulterer be brought to justice through trial and punishment (Numbers 5:11–31; Deuteronomy 22:20–21). The relevant phrase in the Greek can be translated "being a just man, *and* not willing to make her a public example" (KJV), or "being a just man, *but* not willing to make her a publick example" (Anchor Bible; Good News Bible). Either way, that he was tempted to "put her away *privately*" reveals what Joseph's heart was like. To refrain from legally divorcing her—as their espousal required—would make Joseph look bad and likely cause others to assume that Joseph himself had been immoral. Yet, setting his own reputation and embarrassment aside, and not knowing at this point that the baby was from God, Joseph sought to end the relationship in such a way that no one other than the legally required witnesses would know. Thus Mary would be spared *some* of the inevitable embarrassment.[11] As shocked as he might have been at her pregnancy, a potential dilemma for Joseph was that in ancient Judaism the penalty was death for an espoused person who had intimate relations. As John Chrysostom wrote: "To expose and bring her to trial would cause him to deliver her to die. He would do nothing of the sort. So Joseph determined to conduct himself now by a higher rule than the law."[12] Beyond concern for her humiliation, Joseph must have been concerned about whether God would require of him her life. For the law of Moses, to which Joseph sought to be entirely compliant, commanded the death of an adulterer (Deuteronomy 22:20–21).[13]

Not that it would necessarily have added to Joseph's concern, but some gospel scholars, including President J. Reuben Clark, Elder James E. Talmage, and Elder Bruce R. McConkie, believe that Joseph and Mary were cousins. Matthew says Joseph was the son of Jacob, whereas Luke calls him the son of Heli. Apparently, however, Jacob and Heli were brothers, and Heli was the father of Joseph, whereas Jacob was the father of Mary.

This would make Joseph and Mary first cousins with the same ancestral lines.[14] No doubt the paradox in which Joseph found himself drove him to his knees to plead with God for divine intervention. We can only imagine Joseph's feelings of confusion and frustration, and the agony and torment this situation undoubtedly caused him.

Joseph had a significant role to play in the coming forth of the long-awaited messianic era that was about to begin.[15] Mary needed a husband who would be a strong and unwavering witness to her integrity and also a completely trustworthy foster father for our Lord and Savior, who was to be born of her. Joseph was such a husband and earthly father.[16] We can only wonder if this unfathomably difficult circumstance was some divinely dictated test of him who would serve as the earthly stepfather of the Son of God.[17] Yet, of men then dwelling upon the footstool of God, no one greater could be found than Joseph. Robert L. Millet wrote: "Within two short chapters we find Joseph receiving four separate visions in which he was given instructions regarding the birth and protection of Jesus and Mary. Obviously his soul was in tune with the Infinite. This is as it must be, for the stepfather of our Lord had to be capable and ready to receive divine direction."[18] Joseph was the model patriarch, and thus God could use him in this most sacred of mortal callings.

———— • ————

MATTHEW 1:20

*But while he thought on these things, behold,
the angel of the Lord appeared unto him in a
dream, saying, Joseph, thou son of David,
fear not to take unto thee Mary thy wife: for
that which is conceived in her is of the Holy
Ghost.*

The angel of the Lord appeared unto him in a dream

The Joseph Smith Translation changes the wording in
this passage from "dream" to "vision."

Matthew's record is silent on the identity of the
angelic ministrant who appeared to Joseph. Most commentators conjecture that it was Gabriel (that is, Noah),
the same angel who appeared to Mary before the conception of Jesus, but Matthew does not specifically state that
such was the case. Luke speaks of Gabriel appearing
to Mary (Luke 1:26–27) and of the "angel of the Lord"
appearing to the shepherds (Luke 2:9), which may
imply that the two angels were not one and the same.
Like the angel that ministered to the shepherds, Joseph's
ministrant is consistently referred to by Matthew as "the
angel of the Lord."[19] Regardless of who the angel was,

however, what seems most important about the episode is not the identity of the angel but rather the sacred content of the message delivered and the supernally righteous nature of Joseph, which enabled him to receive such a vision.

That which is conceived in her is of the Holy Ghost

The angel assured Joseph that the baby was of God and that Mary had been faithful to him. Clearly, for the time in which they lived, Joseph's marriage to Mary would have been scandalous. People simply did not ignore adultery and infidelity in antiquity. It was a major shame and a serious offense. Joseph, at least initially, had to have been both frightened and embarrassed at all of this.[20] Thus, one fourth-century Church Father wrote:

> While St. Joseph, yet uninformed of so great a mystery, wanted to put away Mary quietly, he was advised in a dream by an angel . . . of the heavenly mystery, lest he think otherwise about Mary's virginity . . . It was not appropriate for so great a mystery to be revealed to anyone other than Joseph, who was known to be Mary's fiancé, and no reproach of sin was attached to his name. In fact, *Joseph* translated from Hebrew into Latin means "beyond reproach."[21]

As already noted, in addition to the fear of what men would think, Joseph likely was afraid lest he give offense to God by retaining as his wife an adulteress, which was contrary to the dictates of the law. But now the vision had come. The prayers had been answered. The knowledge so requisite to Joseph's state of peace was received:

> Joseph now knew! Doubt fled. The circle of true believers was growing. He had the same testimony, from the same source, as did Mary and Elisabeth and Zacharias [that is, by divine revelation]; and, according to their law, in the mouths of two or three witnesses shall every word be established. The Lord was providing his witnesses, and soon the whole nation and the whole world would be bound to believe, and that at the peril of their salvation. How often Joseph bore the special witness that was his we do not know, but that he remained true to every trust and that he performed the mission assigned him by the Lord, there can be no doubt.[22]

———— • ————

MATTHEW 1:21

And she shall bring forth a son, and thou

*shalt call his name JESUS: for he shall save
his people from their sins.*

Thou shalt call his name JESUS: for he shall save his people from their sins

The Greek name *Jesus* (*Yeshua* or *Joshua* in Hebrew) means "Jehovah is salvation" or "the Lord saves." In one verse of scripture (Matthew 1:21)—indeed, in the very name "Jesus"—is recorded the entire reason for Christ's life and ministry. The divinely dictated name says everything about who this child was destined to become and what He had been sent by God to accomplish. He was to be the Great Atoning One.[23]

•

MATTHEW 1:22

Now all this was done, that it might be fulfilled which was spoken of the Lord by the prophet, saying,

That it might be fulfilled which was spoken of the Lord

Naming the child "Jesus" fulfilled prophecy. Though He was not Joseph's own son, the godly carpenter had been called to exhibit a father's care toward the Son of God. On this occasion, at this moment of giving Jesus a name, Joseph stood in significant relation to the babe of Bethlehem and also to the child's true Father, God the Eternal Father.

———— • ————

MATTHEW 1:23

Behold, a virgin shall be with child, and shall bring forth a son, and they shall call his name Emmanuel, which being interpreted is, God with us.

They shall call his name Emmanuel

Matthew quotes the prophecy of Isaiah 7:14, in which we learn that the Messiah would be called "Immanuel." Matthew says "they" (likely indicating Joseph and Mary) "shall call his name Emmanuel" (meaning "God with us"); the Hebrew (in Isaiah 7:14) indicates that His mother would give him that name. That should not be taken to mean literally that Mary would name Jesus "Immanuel." On the contrary, the angel Gabriel commanded Mary and Joseph to do otherwise (Matthew 1:21).

But we look in vain for any commentary explaining how the Virgin Mary said of Jesus, in so many words, "Look at my Son. He is God!" Did she bear witness to that effect? Apparently she did. Are such words recorded in scripture? Not with any degree of clarity. It appears, however, that the point of Isaiah's prophecy, as it pertains to her naming him Immanuel, was that she would testify in her words and actions that He was indeed the Son of God and not, as some assumed, the son of Joseph the carpenter. Mary's comments and behavior at the wedding at Cana seem to fulfill the Isaianic requirement that she would name/call Him "Immanuel." For the most part, and as evidence of her great faith in her Son, it is Mary who provokes the first miracle of Jesus' mortal ministry—and in so doing causes His disciples to believe on Him (John 2:1–11). Thus, in a very real sense, she did call His name Immanuel.

MATTHEW 1:24

Then Joseph being raised from sleep did as the angel of the Lord had bidden him, and took unto him his wife:

Joseph . . . took unto him his wife

Joseph was convinced by the vision to stay with Mary and to accept his divine appointment as the earthly guardian of the Son of God. We can thus assume that

Mary and Joseph were united in their vision and aspiration to serve God. We can say with certainty that because of the way they conducted their lives, each of their children was carefully nurtured to be a true believer in the God of their fathers.

MATTHEW 1:25

And knew her not till she had brought forth her firstborn son: and he called his name JESUS.

Knew her not

The biblical euphemism that he "knew her not" is understood to mean that they did not have intimate relations until after Jesus was born. Contrary to some traditions that speak of Mary as a "perpetual virgin," the scriptures attest that after the birth of Jesus, Mary and Joseph reared a family consisting of sons and daughters (Matthew 12:46; 13:55–56; Mark 3:31–32; Luke 8:19–20; John 2:12; 7:3–5; Acts 1:14; Galatians 1:19). Indeed, Jesus' being referred to as Mary's "firstborn son" (Matthew 1:25; Luke 2:7) implies that Joseph and Mary *did* have children together after Jesus' birth. It is generally accepted that Matthew's Gospel was written years after Jesus' death and thus after Mary had completed having her family.

————— • —————

MATTHEW 2:1

*Now when Jesus was born in Bethlehem
of Judaea in the days of Herod the king,
behold, there came wise men from the east to
Jerusalem,*

Jesus was born . . . in the days of Herod

Herod died in 4 B.C., which would place the date of
Jesus' birth at somewhere between 7 B.C. and 6 B.C. rather
than in the years A.D. 0 or A.D. 1, as many assume.[24]

Wise men from the east

Whereas Matthew's Gospel speaks of the "wise men,"
Luke's record only mentions the "shepherds."

Noteworthy is the fact that the wise men went to
Herod, seeking directions to the residence of the Christ
child *after* Jesus' birth, *after* His presentation in the temple
(which would have been when He was forty days old),
and *after* His family had taken up residence in a home in
Bethlehem.[25] These wise men were not present at the side
of the manger, as popularly depicted in many Nativity
scenes. Their arrival was some time after Jesus was born
and while He was residing in a home. Indeed, it is

conjectured that their arrival was about two or two and a half years after His birth.[26]

The title "wise men" is variously translated "wise men," "astrologers," or "Magi." The Greek word translated "wise men" in the King James Version is the same Greek word used to refer to teachers, priests, physicians, astrologers, seers, interpreters of dreams, soothsayers, sorcerers, and false prophets. Thus, the Greek is no help in isolating who these men were.

They went to Jerusalem, asking where they might find Jesus. Because east is the direction that represents the presence of God or inspiration and influence from God, we have to assume that they were not "sorcerers" or "false prophets." Indeed, because Matthew speaks of them as originating in the East, we assume them to be of God, or sent by God.[27] Elder McConkie wrote:

> To suppose they were members of the apostate religious cult of the *Magi* of ancient Media and Persia is probably false. Rather, it would appear they were true prophets, righteous persons like Simeon, Anna, and the shepherds, to whom Deity revealed that the promised Messiah had been born among men. Obviously they were in possession of ancient prophecies telling of the rise of a new star at his birth. That they did receive revelation for their personal guidance

is seen from the inspired dream in which they were warned not to return to Herod after they had found and worshiped the Son of Mary.[28]

Elsewhere Elder McConkie wrote of them: "One thing is clear. They had prophetic insight. . . . The probability is they were themselves Jews who lived, as millions of Jews then did, in one of the nations to the East."[29]

Why did they not go directly to Bethlehem in their quest to worship the Messiah? Unlike Jerusalem, Bethlehem was a small, unknown city, and the prophecy from which they were working apparently was not that specific.[30]

Curiously, although Alma's statement that Christ would be born "at" Jerusalem (instead of Bethlehem) has been criticized time and again by those who seek to destroy the Church,[31] no such criticisms are leveled against the wise men who went to Jerusalem looking for Him. Neither do critics condemn the angel who speaks of Christ as being born "in the city of David" (Luke 2:11), which was Jerusalem (not Bethlehem).[32] It seems a double standard is applied when some examine the Book of Mormon.

———— • ————

MATTHEW 2:2–3

Saying, Where is he that is born King of the Jews? for we have seen his star in the east,

*and are come to worship him. When Herod
the king had heard these things, he was
troubled, and all Jerusalem with him.*

Where is he that is born King of the Jews?

The wise men approached King Herod, seeking to
know where they could find the Christ child, the promised Messiah of the Jewish people, the King of the Jews.[33]
The Joseph Smith Translation changes "King of the Jews"
to "Messiah of the Jews." That title was no less unsettling
to Herod, since by this time in history the Jews were looking for a political messiah to free them from Rome.

We are informed that the wise men had been led to
Jerusalem by a star which they had seen in the east.
Although neither Matthew nor Luke calls the star "new,"
biblical scholars traditionally acknowledge that it was the
star's newness that likely caused the wise men to notice it.
It is from the Book of Mormon, however, that the phrase
"new star" originates (Helaman 14:5; 3 Nephi 1:21).

————— • —————

JST MATTHEW 3:4 (KJV MATTHEW 2:4)

*And when he had gathered all the chief priests,
and scribes of the people together, he demanded
of them, saying, Where is the place that is writ-*

> *ten of by the prophets, in which Christ should*
> *be born? For he greatly feared, yet he believed*
> *not the prophets.*

He demanded of them, . . . Where is the place . . . in which Christ should be born?

Out of growing fear, Herod consulted the chief priests and scribes. Although the Joseph Smith Translation is clearer than the King James Version, both translations evidence Herod's concern that his throne was about to be taken from him. The Joseph Smith Translation adds, "Where is the place that is written of by the prophets, in which Christ should be born? For he [Herod] greatly feared, yet he believed not the prophets."

The "chief priests" and "scribes" are not identified. Some scholars believe that they were members of the Sanhedrin, the very body that would later seek Jesus' life.

—————— • ——————

MATTHEW 2:5

And they said unto him, In Bethlehem of
Judaea: for thus it is written by the prophet,

In Bethlehem of Judaea

The priests and scribes tell Herod that the prophecy indicated that the Messiah would be born in Bethlehem.

The Joseph Smith Translation changes "the prophet" to "the prophets" (plural). This apparently was not a singular prediction but rather the teaching of multiple prophets. It is possible that Micah 5:2 was one of the passages the priests were drawing on. It reads: "But thou, Bethlehem . . . , though thou be little among the thousands of Judah, yet out of thee shall he come forth unto me that is to be ruler in Israel; whose goings forth have been from of old, from everlasting." More often than not, however, scholars assume that the sources the priests and scribes were working from do not appear in the Old Testament today. It is commonly presumed that those sources have either been lost or removed from the biblical text.

·

JST Matthew 3:6 (KJV Matthew 2:6)

The word of the Lord came unto us, saying,
And thou, Bethlehem, which lieth in the land
of Judea, in thee shall be born a prince,
which art not the least among the princes of
Judea; for out of thee shall come the Messiah,
who shall save my people Israel.

Thou, Bethlehem, . . . in thee shall be born a prince

These scribes or priests quoted a prophecy, or perhaps several, to Herod, detailing the location of the Messiah's birth. The Joseph Smith Translation changes the way the prophecy reads. According to the Prophet's rendering of the verse, Christ would not be a governor—that is, a political power who would rule by virtue of popular vote, as the King James Version has it—rather, He would be a prince, one of royal lineage and having the right to rule by virtue of that lineage, not because of popularity or the will of the people. He would not be sent for "political rule" but for "salvation."

•

MATTHEW 2:7

*Then Herod, when he had privily called the
wise men, enquired of them diligently what
time the star appeared.*

Herod . . . enquired of them diligently what time the star appeared

The reason for Herod's query about the timing of the star's first appearance was, of course, to gauge approximately how old the Christ child would have been at that point.

There is some confusion among commentators about the exact nature of this star—that is, what did Matthew intend his readers to understand by "star"—and who was able to see it? One commentator conjectured:

There seems to have been in Jewish prophecy or legend the knowledge that the Messiah's coming would be heralded by a special appearance of a star. Alfred Edersheim wrote: "There is . . . testimony which seems to us not only reliable, but embodies most ancient Jewish tradition. It is contained in one of the smaller *Midrashim*. . . . The so-called Messiah-Haggadah (*Aggadoth Mashiach*) opens as follows: 'A star shall come out of Jacob. . . . The Son of David cometh, . . . and *the Star shall shine forth from the East, and this is the Star of the Messiah.*'"[34]

The suggestion of this commentator is that the star was a literal physical manifestation of the birth of the Jewish Messiah—a great sign that was expected to be rather universally seen and recognized. Yet the implication of Herod's question about the timing of the appearance of the star is that it was not seen by most, or even many people.[35] Regarding this star, one text notes: "It shines, . . . then disappears only to reappear for the wise men but not for others. . . . As to whether parts of Matthew's narrative represent scriptural hyperbole or are intended to be understood literally, this is left to the reader to determine."[36]

It is common for commentators who interpret the new star as a literal physical astronomical sign to conjecture that it was one of three things: (1) some sort of planetary alignment, such as that of Saturn and Jupiter, which took place in 7 B.C.; (2) a comet, such as Halley's, which appeared early in 12 or 11 B.C.; or (3) a nova, which is a star that, owing to an explosion, appears with extraordinary brightness but only for a short time.

Even though two of these phenomena are known to have taken place in the decade of Christ's birth, there are, nevertheless, two problems with all three popular explanations. First, none of the theories account for the ability of the new star to move and guide the wise men. Second and more important, this new star was not noticed by Herod or the chief priests and scribes before or after the wise men approached Herod (see Matthew 2:7). Indeed, any of the three standard explanations regarding what the new star was would have been noted quite universally.

The early Christian "Protevangelium of James" states that Herod "examined the Magi, saying to them: What sign have you seen in reference to the king that has been born? And the Magi said: *We have seen a star of great size shining among these stars, and obscuring their light, so that the stars did not appear;* and we thus knew that a king has been born to Israel, and we have come to worship him."[37] The description is of a star so bright that it actually obscured the other stars in the sky, making them difficult to see, and yet King Herod, his astrologers, and the priests of the day seemed unaware that this sign had been manifest.

All of this suggests that there might be some alternate explanation of what the new star was or why most failed to notice it. It seems quite puzzling that a people whose lives were so heavily influenced by the stars (they used them for calendering, for their religious cycle, for navigation or directions, etc.) would not notice a new star and the time of its first appearance. It also seems puzzling that the scribes, who copied the scriptures, and the priests, who studied the texts, would not be reminded of the prophecy of the new star as a herald of the coming Messiah, if indeed they saw a new star in the heavens. Thus, it is believed by some scholars (and is implied by Matthew) that the "star" was not universally visible or recognizable and that, quite possibly, the new star was something other than some astrological phenomenon.

———— • ————

MATTHEW 2:8

And he sent them to Bethlehem, and said, Go and search diligently for the young child; and

> *when ye have found him, bring me word*
> *again, that I may come and worship him also.*

He sent them to Bethlehem

Herod instructed the wise men to return and tell him where the boy was so that he could worship the child.[38] Herod did not wish to worship Christ; he wanted to kill Him; but his attempts at deception and murder would be foiled. Herod would be unable to find the Christ child, whom he was seeking. The corrupt king Herod the Great well symbolizes all those today who, falsely seeking after the Lord, never manage to find Him.

---•---

MATTHEW 2:9

> *When they had heard the king, they*
> *departed; and, lo, the star, which they saw in*
> *the east, went before them, till it came and*
> *stood over where the young child was.*

The star . . . went before them

Again, the text suggests that not everyone could see the star. It seems to have appeared and disappeared, contingent upon the audience. It is quite possible that the receptivity of the wise men to the Spirit enabled them to see and recognize the star for what it was—a herald of the messianic age. Certainly Herod and the leaders of the Jews at that time had no such receptivity and thereby seem to have missed both the star and its meaning. Those evil men would have followed the star to the home of Jesus had they been able to see it.

It is also feasible that Matthew's reference to the star was dualistic, for a star was a common ancient symbol for an angel. Indeed, that is exactly how John the Revelator, Abraham, and Isaiah use *star or stars* (see Revelation 1:20; 9:1; Abraham 3:13, 17–18; Isaiah 14:12–13). In other words, perhaps this elusive star represents a literal star[39] or a frequent visitation from some heavenly messenger instructed by the Lord to guide the wise men on their quest.[40] We are told in several of the early Christian infancy narratives that an angel appeared to the wise men and came "in the form of that star" rather than in the form of a man.

——————— • ———————

MATTHEW 2:10–11

When they saw the star, they rejoiced with exceeding great joy. And when they were come into the house, they saw the young child with Mary his mother, and fell down, and worshipped him: and when they had opened

> *their treasures, they presented unto him gifts;*
> *gold, and frankincense, and myrrh.*

They . . . fell down, and worshiped him: and . . .
presented unto him gifts

Some have conjectured that the gifts from the wise men financed the family's extended stay in Egypt. It is certain, however, that the three gifts listed by Matthew symbolize Christ, His nature, and the gifts He would bring to the world. Interpretations of their meanings include the following:

Gold. Representative of the celestial or godly nature of Christ, including His incorruptibility, purity, and wisdom. Gold is also a symbol of royalty, kingship, and power.

Frankincense. Symbolizing sacrifice, communion with God, and resurrection.

Myrrh. A balm related to suffering, healing, anointing, and atonement.

That there were three gifts has provoked the tradition that there were three wise men. The number three, however, represents that which is godly or divine in nature and origin, and it is likely for this reason that there were three gifts—that is, Jesus was godly/divine in His nature and origin and the wise men were sent of God.

—— • ——

MATTHEW 2:12

And being warned of God in a dream that
they should not return to Herod, they
departed into their own country another way.

Being warned of God in a dream

The warning dream sent from God to the wise men helped to preserve Jesus' life and allowed Joseph to move the family to a safe location before Herod could start looking for them. It also indicates that these men were inspired and led of God and highly receptive to His Spirit. Finally, as with Herod, so it is with us—God knows the intents and desires of every man's heart (Hebrews 4:12; Alma 18:32; D&C 6:16).

One early Christian document claims that when the wise men did not return, Herod "sent through all the roads, wishing to seize them and put them to death. But when he could not find them at all, he sent anew to Bethlehem and all its borders, and slew all of the . . . children whom he found of two years old and under."[41]

—— • ——

MATTHEW 2:13–15

And when they were departed, behold, the
angel of the Lord appeareth to Joseph in a

dream, saying, Arise, and take the young
child and his mother, and flee into Egypt,
and be thou there until I bring thee word: for
Herod will seek the young child to destroy
him. When he arose, he took the young child
and his mother by night, and departed into
Egypt: and was there until the death of
Herod: that it might be fulfilled which was
spoken of the Lord by the prophet, saying,
Out of Egypt have I called my son.

Flee into Egypt

The flight into Egypt is one of the many examples of how Christ's life was foreshadowed by the life of the prophet Moses.[42] As to how that flight relates to our own lives, the late fourth-century Church Father John Chrysostom wrote:

There is another lesson also to be learned, which tends powerfully toward true self-constraint in us. We are warned from the beginning to look out for temptations and plots. . . . Thus you see even at his birth a tyrant raging, a flight ensuing and a departure beyond the border. For it was because of no crime that his family was exiled into the land of Egypt.

Similarly, you yourself need not be troubled if you are suffering countless dangers. Do not expect to be celebrated or crowned promptly for your troubles. Instead you may keep in mind the long-suffering example of the mother of the Child, bearing all things nobly, knowing that such a fugitive life is consistent with the ordering of spiritual things. You are sharing the kind of labor Mary herself shared. So did the magi. They both were willing to retire secretly in the humiliating role of fugitive.[43]

Matthew informs us that this midnight flight into Egypt fulfilled the prophecy in which God stated, "Out of Egypt have I called my son" (Matthew 2:15; see also Hosea 11:1).

The Joseph Smith Translation says that the "angel of the Lord appeared to Joseph in a vision." That certainly says something about the prophetic and spiritual gifts of Joseph. Jesus' stepfather was a great, spiritually-in-tune, faithful Saint.

———— • ————

MATTHEW 2:16

Then Herod, when he saw that he was mocked of the wise men, was exceeding

> *wroth, and sent forth, and slew all the chil-*
> *dren that were in Bethlehem, and in all the*
> *coasts thereof, from two years old and under,*
> *according to the time which he had diligently*
> *enquired of the wise men.*

Herod . . . was exceedingly wroth

When the wise men did not return, Herod slew all the babies in Bethlehem and the surrounding region who were two years old or younger. Elder McConkie wrote: "Children are counted as being two years of age until they attain their third birthday."[44] Thus, Herod's death decree fell upon all that were under three years of age. Herod arrived at this age by calculating when the wise men first saw the star. Additionally, although the goal was to kill a specific boy, both males and females may have been slaughtered, as it is highly improbable that the soldiers implementing this death penalty would bother to see what sex a child was before killing it.

This cold massacre of children is in keeping with the character of Herod who, according to Josephus, slew three of his own sons because they were potential rivals to his throne. Augustus Caesar is said to have remarked: "It is better to be Herod's pig than his son"—meaning that because Herod was a Jew, he could not kill and eat his pigs, but his sons were not as safe.

Because of the size of Bethlehem and the surrounding neighborhoods, coupled with the infant mortality rate of the time, scholars believe the total number of children slain was likely low, perhaps even as low as twenty:

> This senseless act, like the decree pronounced anciently by Pharaoh before the birth of Moses (Exodus 1:8–22), dramatizes the paranoid and wicked frenzy that characterized the mind and heart of the ruler ironically designated by history as Herod the Great. This heinous act is but another illustration of Satan's fruitless efforts to thwart the accomplishment of the purposes of God. The Saints of the Most High move forward, despite such opposition, trusting the prophetic promise that "no weapon that is formed against thee shall prosper" (Isaiah 54:17; D&C 71:9).[45]

The possibility of a relatively low number of children slain does not negate the significance of the massacre, but it does serve to put it into historical perspective and explain why no historical texts (outside the Bible) mention the heinous event. Those who lost their lives that morning in Bethlehem, having died on behalf of Christ, became the first martyrs of the New Testament era. Their lives were taken that He might live, just as some thirty years later He would give His life that we might live eternally.

Of Herod and his "fear-driven rage," one author wrote: "Surely such devilish abuse of innocent life through tyrannical force evidences that the battle waged in heaven long ago between the followers of Satan and the disciples of Christ has carried over to Earth."[46]

———— • ————

JST MATTHEW 3:17–18
(KJV MATTHEW 3:17–18)

Then was fulfilled that which was spoken by Jeremiah the prophet, saying, In Ramah there was a voice heard, lamentation, and weeping, and great mourning; Rachael weeping for the loss of her children, and would not be comforted because they were not.

Then was fulfilled that which was spoken by Jeremiah the prophet

Matthew is quoting Jeremiah 31:15, although it is unclear in what sense he sees the passage applying to the slaughter of the infants of Bethlehem. It is possible that Matthew cites the Jeremiah passage because, like Rachael (who was buried near by), the mothers of Bethlehem had reason to mourn and weep.

It is also possible that Matthew intends his readers to know that the Jeremiah passage foretold a positive ending, one in which the children would be returned. If this latter option was Matthew's intent, then his quotation from Jeremiah was meant to instill hope and trust in the Lord. Even though this event was tragic, good would come and blessings would be obtained. One commentary states:

> We have the problem of [not knowing] how Matthew understood Jeremiah. . . . Although Jeremiah describes Rachael as crying for her children [probably a reference to the captivity and deportation of the tribes of the Northern Kingdom by the Assyrians in 722–721 B.C.], God's message to her is to stop weeping and crying, since the children are going to come back from the land of the enemy (31:16–17). In other words this is a message of joy and hope.[47]

—————— • ——————

MATTHEW 2:19–21

But when Herod was dead, behold, an angel of the Lord appeareth in a dream to Joseph in Egypt, saying, Arise, and take the young child and his mother, and go into the land of

> *Israel: for they are dead which sought the*
> *young child's life. And he arose, and took the*
> *young child and his mother, and came into*
> *the land of Israel.*

An angel of the Lord appeareth in a dream to Joseph

Again, the Joseph Smith Translation changes this from a "dream" to a "vision." In this vision Joseph was told to return to his homeland as Herod was dead. The angel uses the plural "they are dead," which appears to refer to Herod and (likely) those who concurred in his decree of death for the infants of Bethlehem (perhaps conspirators, such as the chief priests and scribes).

The revelation came not to Mary but to Joseph, as the patriarch of the home, highlighting the truth that in a very real sense, God the Father had given Joseph stewardship over the infant child. Indeed, the Father had placed Joseph as the protector and provider for two of the greatest and most worthy of all His spirit offspring (Jesus and Mary), which says volumes about Joseph and the Father's feelings about him.

Because Herod died in March of 4 B.C., the date of this vision would likely have been some time between March and April of that same year.

———— • ————

MATTHEW 2:22–23

But when he heard that Archelaus did reign
in Judaea in the room of his father Herod, he
was afraid to go thither: notwithstanding,
being warned of God in a dream, he turned
aside into the parts of Galilee: and he came
and dwelt in a city called Nazareth: that it
might be fulfilled which was spoken by the
prophets, He shall be called a Nazarene.

And he came and dwelt in a city called Nazareth

Joseph headed back to Bethlehem of Judea but upon hearing that Herod's son was reigning as his father's successor in the southern part of Herod's kingdom, Joseph changed his plans and took the family to Nazareth.[48] In so doing, once again, prophecy was fulfilled, though which prophecy Matthew was referring to is unknown. The city of Nazareth is not mentioned in the Old Testament, nor does this prophecy exist in any Old Testament text currently available.[49]

———— • ————

JST MATTHEW 3:24

And it came to pass that Jesus grew up with his

> *brethren, and waxed strong, and waited upon*
> *the Lord for the time of his ministry to come.*

Jesus grew up . . . and waxed strong

Like other Jewish boys, Jesus grew up with His brothers and sisters (Matthew 12:46–47; 13:55; Mark 3:31–32; 6:3; Luke 8:19–20; John 7:3–5). He waited for the appointed time of His ministry to arrive. Matthew's comments imply that Jesus knew from His youth who He was (that is, the Messiah; see Luke 2:52) and what He was destined to do and become.

Also like other Jewish boys of age twelve and older, Jesus would have attended the Passover celebrations in Jerusalem. President J. Reuben Clark Jr. wrote: "We can but wonder what thoughts passed through the mind of the divinely begotten Youth as He saw all this [the preparations in Jerusalem for the annual Feast of the Passover], and realized, as He must, that all of it was, in some measure, symbolic of the sacrifice He Himself was to make."[50] Elder Bruce R. McConkie gives us an idea of the magnitude of those preparations: "In the day of Jesus, both public and private sacrifices were made, and the paschal lambs were slain for each family or group, each of such units containing from ten to twenty persons. When Nero sat in

Caesar's seat a count was made of the number of lambs slain in Jerusalem at one Passover: the total, 256,000."[51]

———— • ————

JST MATTHEW 3:25–26

And he served under his father, and he spake not as other men, neither could he be taught; for he needed not that any man should teach him. And after many years, the hour of his ministry drew nigh.

He spake not as other men

Jesus was in a mortal body, but He was not a mortal. He could be taught by no man because, by the age of twelve, He had already parted the veil and received divine teaching beyond that possessed by any mortal of His day. It will be recalled that the Prophet Joseph Smith stated, if you "gaze into heaven five minutes, you would know more than you would by reading all that ever was written on the subject."[52] By age twelve Jesus had gazed into heaven and thus knew more than all men combined.

CHAPTER THREE

LUKE'S ACCOUNT OF THE BIRTH OF CHRIST

Like Matthew, through his Gospel account Luke bears witness that Jesus is the Christ, the divine Son of God sent from the presence of the Father to save the inhabitants of a fallen world. Both Matthew and Luke share their individual insights into the birth of Christ; however, Luke is much more detailed than is Matthew. If we look only at the total number of verses, Luke gives us nearly 58 percent more than Matthew does, offering some seventy verses of commentary, in comparison to Matthew's thirty. This may have some bearing on why Luke's account has consistently been more popular with those who read the Nativity story at Christmastime.

What follows is a verse by verse examination of Luke's account of Christ's birth as recorded in the King James Version of the Bible (in Luke 1:26–56; 2:1–40) and in the Joseph Smith Translation (in Luke 1:26–56; 2:1–40).[1]

———— • ————

JST LUKE 1:26–28 (KJV LUKE 1:26–28)

*And in the sixth month the angel Gabriel
was sent from God unto a city of Galilee,
named Nazareth, to a virgin espoused to a
man whose name was Joseph, of the
house of David; and the virgin's name was
Mary. And the angel came in unto her and
said, Hail, thou virgin, who art highly
favored of the Lord. The Lord is with thee,
for thou art chosen and blessed among
women.*

The angel Gabriel was sent from God

The angel Gabriel, second only to Michael in the
heavenly angelic hierarchy as it pertains to this earth, was
sent by God to announce the coming of the Messiah.
When living upon the earth as a mortal, Gabriel was the
prophet Noah.

A virgin espoused to a man

See commentary on Matthew 1:18.

The virgin's name was Mary

Mary is an alternate form of Miriam. It is a Semitic name of Hebrew or Canaanite origin and means "height" or "summit," but here probably connotes "excellence." More commonly, the names Miriam and Mary are interpreted as meaning "bitterness." Certainly both definitions could apply to Mary's life. Although her life was one of many transcendant joys, she also had many "bitter" or hard experiences, from the seemingly scandalous pregnancy to the premature death of her husband and (from a mother's perspective) the early death of her son.

And in the sixth month

Elisabeth was in her sixth month of pregnancy with John (the Baptist) when the angel Gabriel appeared to Mary and told her of both Elisabeth's pregnancy and her own future pregnancy. As Elisabeth had remained in seclusion for the first five months of her pregnancy (Luke 1:24–25), Mary was apparently unaware of the miracle that had taken place in the home of Zachariah and his wife.

Hail, thou virgin, who art highly favored of the Lord

Rather than "hail," as the King James Version renders it, the Greek indicates that the angel said to Mary "rejoice," because she was highly favored of God.[2] This greeting does not surprise us. Favored indeed she was. As one modern apostle of the Lord Jesus Christ wrote: "The greatest of all female spirits was the one . . . chosen and foreordained to be 'the mother of the Son of God, after the manner of the flesh.' [1 Nephi 11:18.]"[3] Elsewhere we read:

> Can we speak too highly of her whom the Lord has blessed above all women? There was only one Christ, and there is only one Mary. Each was noble and great in preexistence, and each was foreordained to the ministry he or she performed. We cannot but think that the Father would choose the greatest female spirit to be the mother of his Son, even as he chose the male spirit like unto him to be the Savior. . . . We should . . . hold up Mary with that proper high esteem which is hers.[4]

Mary's favored status came as a direct result of her supernal righteousness in the premortal world and the holy way in which she conducted herself here in this second estate. She who sought to imitate the life of an angel was worthy to enjoy the experience of speaking with an angel.

—————— • ——————

LUKE 1:29–30

And when she saw him, she was troubled at
his saying, and cast in her mind what man-
ner of salutation this should be. And the
angel said unto her, Fear not, Mary: for thou
hast found favour with God.

And when she saw him, she was troubled

Mary's reason for fear was not that she had seen an
angel. "Zechariah had been 'gripped with fear' (V.12) at
the very appearance of the angel, but it was the angel's
words—viz., his greeting (V.28)—that 'greatly troubled'
Mary (V.29)."[5] She was shocked at his claims; indeed, his
announcement that she was "highly favored" of God and
"blessed among women" provoked fear in her. Matthew
Henry noted that Gabriel was saying to Mary, in so many
words, "*you have found favour with God more than you*
think . . . , as there are many who think they are more
favoured of God than really they are."[6] This fear of the
angel's words was simply an evidence of Mary's great
modesty, or humility. She likely felt that such aggrandiz-
ing claims regarding her character were overstated and
thus inappropriate.

———— • ————

LUKE 1:31–33

And, behold, thou shalt conceive in thy
womb, and bring forth a son, and shalt call
his name JESUS. He shall be great, and shall
be called the Son of the Highest: and the
Lord God shall give unto him the throne of
his father David: and he shall reign over the
house of Jacob for ever; and of his kingdom
there shall be no end.

Thou shalt conceive . . . a son . . . called the Son of the
Highest

Unlike Matthew, who speaks of the baby as being conceived "of the Holy Ghost," Luke simply states that Mary will conceive a son who will be called "the Son of the Highest." Luke's statement has provoked much less speculation and confusion than has Matthew's (see commentary on Matthew 1:18).

Thou . . . shalt call his name Jesus

For an explanation of the meaning of the name *Jesus,* see the commentary on Matthew 1:21.

God shall give unto him the throne of his father David

The anticipated Messiah of the Jewish people was expected to come from the lineage of David (2 Samuel 7:12–29; Psalm 89:29).[7] Because of the apostate condition of the Jewish people, however, they would reject their Messiah and God. Gabriel's words are noteworthy. He said to Mary: "God shall give unto him the throne of his father David" (Luke 1:32). It was not the Jewish people but God who would give Jesus Christ the right to rule and reign. Regardless of whether or not the Jews accepted Him, the work of God would roll forth. As the Prophet Joseph stated:

> No unhallowed hand can stop the work from progressing; persecutions may rage, mobs may combine, armies may assemble, calumny may defame, but the truth of God will go forth boldly, nobly, and independent, till it has penetrated every continent, visited every clime, swept every country, and sounded in every ear, till the purposes of God shall be accomplished, and the Great Jehovah shall say the work is done.[8]

If that is true of the restoration of the gospel of Jesus Christ, then it is even more true of Him who made effectual the Father's plan of salvation, taught the gospel, and wrought that infinite and eternal sacrifice upon which all mankind are dependent. Rejection of Christ only ensures the damnation of those who refuse Him. It does little to hinder the work of Him whom God has sent.

He shall reign over the house of Jacob for ever; and of his kingdom there shall be no end

In Jesus' day it was generally believed that the Messiah's kingdom would be of a limited duration because no man (in a mortal sense) lives forever. But Jesus was not sent to establish an earthly, temporal kingdom. It was the politics of God, not those of man, that Gabriel referred to. Thus, when the postmortal Noah speaks of the permanence of Jesus' kingdom, he is speaking of a spiritual or heavenly reign. During His mortal ministry, Jesus never sought His place on the earthly throne of David.

•

JST LUKE 1:34–38 (KJV LUKE 1:34–38)

Then said Mary unto the angel; How can this be? And the angel answered and said unto her, Of the Holy Ghost, and the power of the Highest. Therefore also, that holy child that shall be born of thee shall be called the Son of God. And behold, thy cousin Elisabeth, she hath also conceived a son, in her old age; and this is the sixth month with her who is called barren. For with God nothing can be impossible. And Mary said, Behold the handmaid of the Lord; be it unto me according to thy word. And the angel departed from her.

How can this be?

The King James Version implies that Mary's question to Gabriel was, in essence, "How can I have a baby if I'm not legally and lawfully wedded? I have no husband, and I am a virgin, so how am I going to have a child?" This seems a strange question to ask, because she was already betrothed to Joseph and thus, they would be living together as husband and wife within the year. One wonders why she did not assume that the conception would occur after her marriage. Thus, in the King James Version Mary's question is puzzling.

The Joseph Smith Translation, however, resolves the problem. It drops the phrase "seeing I know not a man," implying, perhaps, that Mary's question was not about how she could conceive a child but about her already being engaged to be married and the Messiah was to be born of a virgin (Isaiah 7:14), so she could not qualify to be the mother of the Messiah. She would only be a virgin for, at best, one more year (the length of the average espousal) and then would consummate her marriage with the man to whom she was already contractually espoused. The issue in her mind would not have been that she was a virgin and thus could not conceive but rather that she was a woman about to be married and thus could not have a virgin birth, as required by ancient prophecy. That is why she asks, "How can this be?" (JST Luke 1:34).

According to Ambrose (a fourth-century bishop of Milan), unlike Zacharias's question, Mary's asking, "How can this be?" was not a sign of disbelief in the angel's words but rather a query for understanding.[9] Zacharias, on the other hand, specifically asked Gabriel by what sign he would know that the words the angel was telling him were true (Luke 1:18).

Of the Holy Ghost, and the power of the Highest

For a discussion of the role of the Holy Ghost in the begetting of Jesus, see the commentary on Luke 1:31–33 and Matthew 1:18.

Thy cousin Elisabeth

Although the King James Version calls Elisabeth Mary's "cousin," other translations normally render the Greek "kinswoman" or "relative." The actual meaning of the Greek root is rather broad. It can mean a relative of unspecified closeness. The degree of family relationship implied by the Greek is vague. It can mean a neighbor, someone from the same village, someone from the same tribe, or someone with the same political or national affiliations.[10] Even in the King James Version of the Bible, of the twelve times this particular Greek word is translated, only in two of those is it translated "cousin"—and in both of those instances it is used regarding Elisabeth.

The Protestant reformer John Wycliffe popularized the idea that "cousin" was the intended meaning of the Greek. Mary and Elisabeth may have been blood relatives or they may have simply been close friends from the same city or tribe of Israel. Similarly, John the Baptist and Jesus may not have actually been cousins, but if they were, they could have been no closer than second cousins.

In the end, it matters little. The two women were obviously close.

With God nothing can be impossible

The announcement that Elisabeth, barren and well beyond the age of childbearing, was now in her sixth month of pregnancy places in context the angel's proclamation that "nothing can be impossible" for God (JST Luke 1:37). It is also a fitting conclusion for the discussion between Mary and Gabriel, in which this chosen vessel is told things beyond the comprehension of any mortal.

> This news [regarding Elisabeth] was to be a sign to Mary of the truth of the greater message that had preceded it. Elisabeth, stricken in years and past the childbearing age, was to have a child, because with God nothing is impossible, even as Sarah, also stricken in years and past the childbearing age, was promised a son by the Lord, who said: "Is any thing too hard for the Lord?" (Gen. 18:14.) Gabriel's announcement about Elisabeth was unspoken counsel to Mary to go and receive comfort and help from [Elisabeth], whom she no doubt loved and revered—the inference is that Mary's mother was dead—and who, being herself with child in a miraculous manner, could speak peace to the young virgin's heart as no other mortal could.[11]

In light of all Mary would shortly be called to endure, Elisabeth's miracle would deepen the bond between her and Mary and enable the wife of Zacharias to function as a pillar of strength to the soon-to-be mother of Israel's Messiah.

Be it unto me according to thy word

Of Mary's submissive answer to Gabriel—and more particularly, to the Lord's request of her—one commentator wisely noted:

> We are apt to take this [response] as the most natural thing and accordingly we miss Mary's quiet heroism. She was not yet [fully] married to Joseph. His reaction to her pregnancy might have been expected to be a strong one and Matthew tells us that he did in fact think of divorcing her (Mt. 1:19). Again, while the death penalty for adultery (Dt. 22:23f) does not seem to have been carried out often, it was still there. Mary could not be sure that she would not have to suffer, perhaps even die. But she recognized the will of God and accepted it.[12]

In addition, Elder Bruce R. McConkie wrote:

> Then Mary gave the answer that ranks, in submissive obedience and divine conformity, along with the one given by the Beloved and Chosen One in the councils of eternity. When he was chosen to be the Redeemer and to put into operation the terms and conditions of his Father's plan, he said: "Father, thy will be done, and the glory be thine

forever." (Moses 4:2.) Mary said simply: "Behold
the handmaid of the Lord; be it unto me according
to thy word."[13]

Actually, Mary seems not just content or resigned that
it should be so but humbly desires that it may be so.
There is a lesson to be learned in this. Like Mary, we
should ground our hopes and desires in the word and will
of God and with her say, particularly in our times of trial
or testing, "Be it unto me according to thy word." Elaine
Cannon wrote: "Reading between the lines one senses the
sweetness, wonder, and faith of Mary. . . . In humility she
submitted her will, her life, to Deity's plan. Perhaps her
Divine Son is not the only one in that sacred family from
whom we have much to learn about obedience."[14]

———— • ————
LUKE 1:39–40

And Mary arose in those days, and went into
the hill country with haste, into a city of
Juda; And entered into the house of
Zacharias, and saluted Elisabeth.

Mary . . . went . . . with haste

One might ask why Mary went with haste to the
home of Elisabeth. Some commentators have thought

that it was to prevent neighbors at Nazareth from knowing about her own pregnancy. Others have suggested, however, that the meaning of the Greek simply implies that she went "with serious intent" or with "eagerness." Additionally, it is possible that her haste is simply a reflection of her desire to be obedient to the plan revealed to her by the angel Gabriel. In the end, it is certain that whatever Mary's reason, it was *not* to see if what the angel had said about Elisabeth was true. In other words, Mary did not go because of any doubts.

———— • ————

LUKE 1:41–45

And it came to pass, that, when Elisabeth heard the salutation of Mary, the babe leaped in her womb; and Elisabeth was filled with the Holy Ghost: and she spake out with a loud voice, and said, Blessed art thou among women, and blessed is the fruit of thy womb. And whence is this to me, that the mother of my Lord should come to me? For, lo, as soon as the voice of thy salutation sounded in mine ears, the babe leaped in my womb for joy. And blessed is she that believed: for there shall be a

> *performance of those things which were told*
> *her from the Lord.*

The babe leaped in her womb

John's foreordained mission was to "go before the face of the Lord to prepare his ways" (Luke 1:76). He was the Elias sent to prepare the way, both through his administering the ordinance of baptism and through his unyielding testimony that Jesus is the Christ (John 3:25–36). One fourth-century bishop wrote:

> Not yet born, already John prophesies and, while yet still in the enclosure of his mother's womb, confesses the coming of Christ with movements of joy. . . . Before his eyes can see what the world looks like, he can recognize the Lord of the world with his spirit. . . . Thus we ought not to marvel that after Herod put him in prison, he continued to announce Christ to his disciples from his confinement, when even confined in the womb he preached the same Lord by his movements.[15]

The leaping of John in the womb of his mother serves to establish his foreordained prophetic mantle and attest to the accuracy of Christ's pronouncement: "Among them that are born of women there hath not risen a greater [prophet] than John the Baptist" (Matthew 11:11).

Elisabeth was filled with the Holy Ghost: and she spake out with a loud voice

Perhaps inspired by her yet-to-be-born son's reaction, Elisabeth spoke prophetically: "Blessed art thou among women, and blessed is the fruit of thy womb."

Blessed art thou among women

The phrase "blessed art thou among women" can mean literally "you are the most blessed of all women." We should note the complete absence of any jealousy in Elisabeth's attitude toward Mary. The older of the two women, who had herself been the recipient of a most significant blessing from the Lord, in genuine humility recognized the supreme nature of the honor God had given to Mary.

Blessed is the fruit of thy womb

Although Luke does not tell us when the conception took place, it is quite clear, both from this statement and John's response to Mary, that she was already pregnant with Jesus Christ.

Whence is this . . . that the mother of my Lord should come to me?

Elisabeth's asking why the mother of her Lord should come to her shows that Elisabeth recognized through the Holy Spirit both that Mary was the mother of the coming Messiah and also that Jesus (yet unborn) would be Elisabeth's Redeemer and the Savior of the world.

Beyond that, commentators tend to see in Elisabeth's words the typological fulfillment of an event recorded in the book of 2 Samuel:

> Luke's words echo the story of II Samuel 6 where David takes the ark (in which according to Hebrew thought, Num. 10:35, was the very presence of God) to the house of Obed-Edom for three months while on the way to Jerusalem. The [Old Testament] 'narrative is an account, in an historical form, of the festival which was held to mark the installation of David as king in Jerusalem. Similarly, Mary carries the Christ [the rightful heir to the Davidic throne], and the narrative will bring them soon to Jerusalem [but first Mary will stay three months at Elisabeth's just as the ark stayed three months in the house of Obed-Edom]; and just as then the crowds rejoiced and David leaped, now Elisabeth rejoices and the babe leaps in the womb.[16]

Related to this same metaphor is Luke's speaking of the "power of the Highest" overshadowing Mary, language that reminds us of Jehovah's "overshadowing" the Mosaic tabernacle and ark of the covenant (Exodus 40:35; Numbers 9:18–22).

And blessed is she that believed

Elisabeth added her personal witness that all the angel Gabriel had told Mary would indeed come to pass. As one commentator put it, "Elisabeth gave the blessing Zachariah's muteness prevented him from giving."[17] From this prophetic declaration it appears that Elisabeth knew the details of that which had been promised to Mary before her arrival at Elisabeth's home.

It is also possible that Elisabeth was drawing a comparison between Mary and Zacharias—the former who believed all that was told her and the latter who wished some proof that the unbelievable would indeed come to pass.

—— • ——

LUKE 1:46–56

*And Mary said, My soul doth magnify the
Lord, and my spirit hath rejoiced in God my
Saviour. For he hath regarded the low estate*

*of his handmaiden: for, behold, from hence-
forth all generations shall call me blessed. For
he that is mighty hath done to me great
things; and holy is his name. And his mercy is
on them that fear him from generation to generation. He hath shewed strength with his
arm; he hath scattered the proud in the imagination of their hearts. He hath put down the
mighty from their seats, and exalted them of
low degree. He hath filled the hungry with
good things; and the rich he hath sent empty
away. He hath holpen his servant Israel, in
remembrance of his mercy; as he spake to our
fathers, to Abraham, and to his seed for ever.
And Mary abode with her about three
months, and returned to her own house.*

Mary said, My soul doth magnify the Lord

Luke 1:46–56 is traditionally known as "Mary's
Song," or the "Magnificat," which is derived from the first
word of the Latin version of this song and means literally
to "enlarge." Here Mary "enlarges" or "aggrandizes" God
by ascribing to Him greatness. In other words, these verses
represent Mary's testimony to Elisabeth—and, in a sense,
to the world—of what God has done for her, how He

vindicates the downtrodden, and how He ministers to the hungry.

This section of scripture is saturated with phrases and concepts from the Hebrew Bible and cites no fewer than twelve different passages. It is strong evidence of Mary's deep piety and detailed knowledge of scripture, as would be expected of the one chosen to nurture and rear the Son of God.

My soul doth magnify the Lord, and my spirit hath rejoiced in God my Saviour

Mary spoke her feelings of gratitude for her Savior, which caused her to praise, or "magnify," Him.[18] One third-century Christian text noted that the "magnification" of the Lord is not a reference to God undergoing "increase" or "loss." On the contrary, the "magnification" of the Lord happens when the sons and daughters of God, like Mary, determine to shape their lives "into the image of Christ" rather than "the form of the devil."[19] It is very much like Alma's query: "Have ye received his image in your countenances?" (Alma 5:14).

He hath regarded the low estate of his handmaiden

Mary spoke of her "low estate," or her humble station. Some have even seen this passage as a reference to her low social position. More particularly, overwhelmed at her role in one of the greatest miracles of all human history, Mary expressed her feelings of unworthiness to be the mother of the Messiah, the Son of God. Here Luke offers us a contrast—Mary's humble mortal station in comparison to the greatness of Almighty God.

> These prophetic words spoken by Mary constitute a remarkable prophecy. The time was about 6 B.C.; the place, an obscure village . . . The speaker, a girl perhaps in her early teens, one of no social standing, and having no claim to fortune. Yet the prophecy is that her name will be had in honorable remembrance by all generations that follow. We know of but one other prophecy that can match this in its improbability and its audacity, that being the prophetic words spoken by the angel Moroni to the youthful Joseph Smith, wherein he was told that his name would be known for both good and evil among those of every nation, kindred, tongue, and people (see Joseph Smith History 1:33). Joseph's situation in life was equally obscure with that of Mary, and the possibility of this prophecy being fulfilled was at the time equally unlikely.[20]

All generations shall call me blessed

All generations would count her as "blessed," not because of any intrinsic, personal holiness or merit— although no greater daughter of God could be found. Rather, they would proclaim her as "blessed" because of Him whom she bore. As one medieval text noted: "She demonstrates that in her own judgement she was indeed Christ's humble handmaid, but with respect to heavenly grace she [acknowledges that] . . . her preeminent blessedness would be marveled at by the voices of all nations."[21] This was hardly a boast on Mary's part. On the contrary! Her words indicate that, if anything, she is humbled beyond comprehension because of this calling and her overwhelming feelings of inadequacy and unworthiness.

His mercy is on them that fear him from generation to generation

While Mary acknowledged her immensely blessed state, she also announced that God is no respecter of persons (Acts 10:34–35). All who fear—that is, reverence and obey—God can lay claim upon His blessings (Psalm 103:17–18). Mary saw herself as but a prototype of the blessed believer.

Through the life, teachings, and sacrifice of the Lord

Jesus Christ, all who fear God become recipients of His mercy—His healing mercy, His forgiving mercy, His comforting mercy, His exalting mercy "from generation to generation."

Shewed strength . . . scattered the proud

One biblical scholar wrote: "This section of the song [vv. 51–54] tells of a complete reversal of human values. It is not *the proud* or *the mighty* or *the rich* who have the last word. Indeed, through his Messiah, God is about to overthrow all these. . . . Mary sings of a God who is not bound by what people do. He turns human attitudes and orders of society upside down."[22]

In Luke 1:51 Mary proclaims that God has given His strength to those who love and reverence Him but has scattered those who are prideful in their hearts. "The proud look down on others because they do not look up to God."[23]

Put down the mighty . . . exalted them of low degree

The "mighty" were the political leaders and aristocracy of Mary's day who would function as rivals to God. Those of "low degree" were the humble people that the "mighty" oppressed, abused, and used for their own gain. Mary's words, of course, span time and are certainly not intended to have application only in her day.

Filled the hungry . . . the rich he hath sent empty away

It was a common idea in the Hebrew Bible that the fortunes of the wicked (often classed as the wealthy) would be taken from them (Job 15:29; Jeremiah 17:11). Here we are told that the divine reversal of the human condition continues. Augustine queried: "Who are the hungry? The humble, the needy. Who are the rich? Proud and self-important people."[24]

He hath holpen his servant Israel

The birth of Jesus, the Davidic heir and Messiah, was evidence that God was indeed coming to the aid of His people: covenant Israel—all who look to God, believe in Him, and seek to keep His words by following His anointed prophets.

Mary abode with her about three months

It is assumed by most New Testament scholars that just before John's birth Mary returned to the home in which she was reared—and, no doubt, to a discussion with Joseph of the sacred events that had transpired since they last spoke.

It seems a little strange that Mary would leave just before Elisabeth gave birth to John, as this would be the time when Mary would be needed most. However, one can only assume that the timing of Mary's departure was dictated by the Spirit, just as was the timing of her visit to Elisabeth. It is possible that Mary went back to Galilee because Joseph sent for her.

———— • ————

LUKE 2:1–5

And it came to pass in those days, that there went out a decree from Caesar Augustus, that all the world should be taxed. (And this taxing was first made when Cyrenius was governor of Syria.) And all went to be taxed, every one into his own city. And Joseph also went up from Galilee, out of the city of Nazareth, into Judaea, unto the city of David, which is called Bethlehem; (because he was of the house and lineage of David:) to be taxed with Mary his espoused wife, being great with child.

All the world should be taxed

Caesar Augustus, the great-nephew of Julius Caesar and ruler of the Roman world in the days of Christ's birth, called for a census (not taxing) of his empire, including Palestine.[25] Joseph, being of the lineage of

David, had to travel to Bethlehem (not Jerusalem) to participate in this census. Joseph had been living in the city of Nazareth, in the province of Galilee. Bethlehem, in the province of Judea, was about five miles south-southwest of Jerusalem. A trek from Nazareth to Bethlehem would be about eighty-five miles if one took the most direct route through Samaria, although it is doubtful (given the cultural and religious antagonism between the Jews and the Samaritans) that Joseph would have gone that way.

Luke speaks of Joseph as going "up" to Bethlehem, when that small village was south of Galilee. But "up" here does not mean northward; rather, it means that Joseph and Mary went "up" in elevation, because Bethlehem was some 734 feet higher than Galilee.

As mentioned earlier, *Bethlehem* means "house of bread," and appropriately so, because it was the birthplace of Jesus, the "Bread of Life."

His espoused wife

As noted above, espousal was akin to a legally binding marriage without the marital intimacy (see commentary on Matthew 1:18). Because of Luke's language, it is believed by some that Joseph and Mary had still not entered into the final stage of marriage by the time Jesus was born—the stage that permitted and made legal the sexual union of husband and wife.[26] Various commentators assume that the formal marriage ceremony took place some time after the birth of Christ.

————————— • —————————

LUKE 2:6–7

And so it was, that, while they were there, the days were accomplished that she should be delivered. And she brought forth her firstborn son, and wrapped him in swaddling clothes, and laid him in a manger; because there was no room for them in the inn.

She brought forth her firstborn son . . . and laid him in a manger

The Messiah was born in a cave or pen used for feeding animals, not in a barn. The Greek word translated "manger" actually means a feeding trough for animals. One text notes:

The only available place for the little family was one usually occupied by animals. It may have been a cave, as tradition suggests. . . . The eating trough, or "manger," was ideal for use as a crib. Luke does not seem to be portraying . . . [the] innkeeper as villain. Rather, he is establishing a contrast between the proper rights of the Messiah in his own "town of David" and the very ordinary and humble circumstances of his birth. . . . Even in his birth Jesus was excluded from the normal shelter others enjoyed.[27]

Some have thought that the birth of Jesus likely took place in the open air, possibly the courtyard of the inn, that being where a manger or feeding trough would likely have been. In the humblest of circumstances God's condescension was witnessed as His Son, the Holy One of Israel, left the courts of glory and came down to earth, taking a tabernacle of clay and becoming the most helpless of all forms of life—a human infant. And for that one night the most natural and humblest of dwellings, a cave, was "made like a temple . . . on account of the birth of the Lord Christ."[28]

Christ was placed like feed in a manger. We who through our sins behave less like children of God and more like animals can partake of the Bread of Life in the hope of sustaining and renewing our spiritual lives.

Wrapped him in swaddling clothes

In contrast to Matthew, Luke the physician informs us that Mary wrapped Jesus in "swaddling" clothes. These clothes consisted of strips of cloth tied together so as to be wrapped around an individual as one would wrap a wound in a gauze bandage. Indeed, the Hebrew word, of which "swaddling" is the English translation, denotes cloths used in the binding of broken limbs (Ezekiel 30:21). This symbolically relates to Christ's ministry of healing the spiritually broken (Ezekiel 34:15–16; D&C 138:42). The use of swaddling clothes evokes two images.

First is the representation of parental care and compassion. These bands provided the child with warmth, protection from extremes of temperature, and a sense of security. As this pertains to Christ, certainly the Father was ever watching over His Firstborn Son. In the end, however, it is Christ who warms, protects, and offers security to us. It is Christ to whom numerous nurturing emblems are applied (Luke 13:34; 3 Nephi 10:6; D&C 10:65). It is Christ who is the Father of our salvation and who entered Gethsemane that He might "know according to the flesh how to succor his people according to their infirmities" (Alma 7:12). Numerous commentators, ancient and modern, have seen significance in the Savior's first clothing. For example, Gregory Thaumaturgus, a third-century Alexandrian Father, wrote: "She wrapped in swaddling-clothes Him who is covered with light as with a garment (Psalm 104:2). She wrapped in swaddling-clothes Him who made every creature. . . . She wrapped Him in swaddling-clothes who binds the whole creation fast with His word."[29] Presbyterian commentator Matthew Henry wrote: "He was wrapped in cloths . . . as if he could be bound, or needed to be kept straight."[30]

Second is the resemblance of swaddling clothes to the clothing of the deceased. Luke's emphasis on Christ's having been wrapped in these strips (commonplace in the world of a physician) may have been to emphasize that this child was born to die. One source noted, "The bonds uniting life with death, where man is concerned, are represented by swaddling clothes (echoed by the bandages that swaddle a corpse)."[31] The language used to describe the scene of Jesus' birth seems deliberate and calculated to foreshadow His death. Jesus is said to be wrapped in cloth strips and placed in a manger (or in a cave) because there was no room for Him in the inn. But upon His death we are told that He was wrapped in linen cloths and placed in a rock-hewn tomb, where no one had yet been laid. Clearly, the language of His birth mirrors or foreshadows the language of His death.

In his homily on Luke 2:41–42, Ambrose, the fourth-century bishop of Milan, wrote: "He was wrapped in swaddling clothes, so that you may be freed from the snares of death. He was in a manger, so that you may be in the [temple]. He was on earth that you may be in the stars. He has no other place in the inn, so that you may have many mansions in the heavens. 'He, being rich, became poor for your sakes, that through his poverty you might be rich' (2 Cor. 8:9)."[32]

There was no room for them in the inn

Of Joseph and Mary's inability to find lodging, one commentator wrote: "The often quoted statement that 'there was no room for them in the inn' can be read to say that there may have been room for others, but not for them. The Joseph Smith Translation renders the text 'inns,' which strengthens that suspicion."[33] As there is no obvious reason for the innkeepers eighty-five miles from Joseph and Mary's home to feel hostility toward the couple, perhaps they simply arrived late, thereby finding accommodations sparse. Certainly Mary's condition would have made their travel slow and difficult.

———— • ————

LUKE 2:8

And there were in the same country shepherds

*abiding in the field, keeping watch over their
flock by night.*

There were in the same country shepherds

Whereas Matthew highlights the wise men who came
to see the Christ child, Luke informs us about the
shepherds, who were out with their flocks on the night of
Christ's birth. Because of the very fact that the shepherds
and sheep were out at night, the appearance of the angel is
not likely to have taken place in December. One text reasons:

The biological rhythm of sheep, like that of
other animals, is influenced by the seasons of the
year. The lambing season occurs in the spring. In
the Middle East sheep drop their lambs within a
period of about two weeks from late March to early
April. During this season the flocks require the constant attention of their keepers. During lambing, for
the safety of their flocks and preservation of the
newborn, shepherds keep careful watch over their
sheep. At no other time in the year are shepherds
more closely tied to their flocks. . . . Only in the
spring, during the lambing season, are shepherds
anxious about the lives of their sheep—so anxious
that they keep watch over their flocks throughout

the night. Many pilgrims in Bethlehem during the middle of winter have been struck by the coldness of the Judean nights. At that time of year the hills and valleys are in the grip of frost, and there are few, if any, shepherds keeping watch over their flocks by night. The sheep are protected from the cold in simple shelters, or have been taken south to the desert. . . . Judean shepherds can be found in the fields keeping watch over their sheep any time from mid-March to early November. . . . Considering how the seasons of the year affect the behavior of the sheep and the shepherds, it seems reasonable to conclude that the shepherds in the hills of Judea would be "keeping watch over their flocks by night" (Luke 2:8) in the spring of the year and that, therefore, spring was a likely time for the birth of Christ.[34]

Commentators frequently point out that Christ's birth was made known to both the wise men (symbolizing the wealthy and privileged of the world) and the shepherds (representing the lowly, humble, and poor). Yet, of the two classes, it was to the poor and the outcast that the message was first given. Perhaps there is a lesson in this regarding Christ's rejection of class distinctions.

In addition, one commentator rhetorically asked:

To whom, we might ask, should the announcement first be made that the King of the Jews had been born? Should those "glad tidings of great joy" be announced first in the court of King Herod, the cruel and wicked tyrant who wrongfully held that office? Or should the announcement of the birth of the Savior of all mankind have been made first in the throne room of mighty Caesar Augustus, himself heralded as a god? Or should it have been made to the presiding high priest of the temple—the Caiaphas of the day? Or among the Pharisees, who so zealously protected the law and then used it as the excuse to reject the Christ? Or what of the Sadducees, who despite their hatred of the Pharisees would join hands with them in seeking the blood of Christ; should it have gone first to them? And what of the Essenes, who cursed their enemies and awaited the day of their power in their desert refuge at Qumran—was it for *them* to entertain angels? How perfect the wisdom of heaven that such an announcement be made first to those who best understood the responsibility of tending the Lord's flock![35]

For what specific purpose were *these* sheep kept? It is traditionally understood that they were raised to be offered as temple sacrifices, their lives to be taken as a typological representation of the atoning sacrifice of the

Only Begotten Son of God. These sheep themselves were symbols of the very Messiah their shepherds were invited to see.

> The Messiah, whose birth was announced to these shepherds, would someday die at the time of the three o'clock afternoon sacrifice, making it no longer necessary for sheep such as theirs to die for people's sins. The Lamb of God had come to die once and for all, so that lambs such as these would not need to die again. No wonder the angel announced the birth of the Messiah to these shepherds![36]

---•---

LUKE 2:9

And, lo, the angel of the Lord came upon them, and the glory of the Lord shone round about them: and they were sore afraid.

The angel of the Lord came . . . and they were sore afraid

These shepherds must have been sincere, faithful, and upright seekers of truth. Their worthiness is implied in their ability to have such a vision. Of them, Elder Bruce R. McConkie wrote: "These were not ordinary shepherds nor ordinary flocks. . . . The shepherds, . . . for whom the veil was then rent . . . were in spiritual stature like Simeon and Anna and Zacharias and Elisabeth and Joseph and the growing group of believing souls who were coming to know, by revelation, that the Lord's Christ was now on earth."[37]

The glory of the Lord shone round about them

The Greek implies a brightness, splendor, or brilliance surrounded the shepherds. That may in part explain their great fear. Luke says that they were "sore afraid." The Greek is "struck with great fear." And who wouldn't be?

---•---

LUKE 2:10

And the angel said unto them, Fear not: for, behold, I bring you good tidings of great joy, which shall be to all people.

Fear not . . . I bring you good tidings

The angel told the shepherds that they should not fear, as the news he brought would bring joy to all people. The Greek phrase, translated in the King James Version as "I bring you good tidings," is literally "I bring you *good news.*" The word *gospel* means, literally, "good news." The angel announced to the shepherds that the gospel was about to be restored and the Law fulfilled to bring joy to all people. Christ is that joy, and eventually *all* will be grateful for what He has done.

———— • ————

LUKE 2:11

For unto you is born this day in the city of David a Saviour, which is Christ the Lord.

Unto you is born this day . . . a Saviour

The angel informed the shepherds that a "Saviour" had been born that day in the City of David. Jesus was actually born about five miles south of the City of David (Jerusalem), in Bethlehem (for a detailed discussion of the angelic use of the phrase "city of David" in reference to Bethlehem, see the commentary on Matthew 2:1).

———— • ————

LUKE 2:12

And this shall be a sign unto you; Ye shall find the babe wrapped in swaddling clothes, lying in a manger.

Ye shall find the babe wrapped in swaddling clothes, lying in a manger

For a discussion of the symbolism of "swaddling clothes," see the commentary on Luke 2:6–7.

The Joseph Smith Translation changes the passage from "this shall be a sign" to "this is the way you shall find" Him. In addition, the shepherds are not instructed to follow a star, as the wise men had been. Rather, they are given details that will help them recognize the Christ child when they see Him (for a discussion of the star that the wise men saw, and potential reasons why the shepherds are not counseled to follow that star, see the commentary on Matthew 2:7 and 9).

LUKE 2:13–14

And suddenly there was with the angel a
multitude of the heavenly host praising God,
and saying, Glory to God in the highest, and
on earth peace, good will toward men.

There was with the angel a multitude of the heavenly host

Whereas one angel had been speaking with the shepherds up to this point, now the angelic hosts join in praising God. They are called a "host," which means, literally, "an army." It is paradoxical that God has an army announce the coming of peace, even the Prince of Peace.

In the King James Version and Joseph Smith Translation

the angels say "glory to God," "peace on earth," and "good will toward mankind." The Greek for this verse is slippery enough that commentators and translators have rendered the passage variously and with multiple connotations:

Glory to God in the highest, and on earth peace to men on whom his favor rests. (New International Version)

Glory to God in the highest heaven, and on earth peace among those whom he favors. (New Revised Standard Version)

Glory to God in high heaven, and peace on earth for men whom he favors! (Moffatt Translation)

Glory to God in the highest heaven, and peace on earth to those with whom he is pleased. (Good News Bible)

Glory to God in the highest heaven, and peace to men who enjoy his favor. (Jerusalem Bible)

Glory in the highest to God, and upon earth peace, among men—good will. (Young's Literal Translation)

Glory in the heights above to God, and upon earth peace among men of good will. (New World Translation)

These alternate translations provide at least two insights absent from the King James Version or the Joseph Smith Translation. First, God is frequently spoken of as dwelling in the "highest heaven" rather than simply dwelling "on high" or receiving the "highest" praise. Second, more often than not, translators see "peace" as being something the angels announced as a gift from God to those whom He "favors" or is "pleased" with. In other words, the angels imply that true peace will not be found in the world except in and through Christ. To obey His law and keep His commandments will bring both divine favor and true inner peace. Thus, the event brought peace to the hearts of Simeon and Anna but not to Herod. The offering is of peace but *only* to those who acknowledge the birth of Christ.

LUKE 2:15–16

And it came to pass, as the angels were gone away from them into heaven, the shepherds said one to another, Let us now go even unto Bethlehem, and see this thing which is come to pass, which the Lord hath made known unto us. And they came with haste, and found Mary, and Joseph, and the babe lying in a manger.

As the angels were gone . . . the shepherds . . . came with haste

With only the sketchy details Luke records, it is unclear how the shepherds knew exactly where to find Jesus. The text has the angel telling them basically that Jesus is near Bethlehem, He will be wrapped in strips of cloth, and they would find Him lying in a feeding trough.

The excitement with which they dropped everything and hurriedly sought the Master reminds us of the Lord's dictate: "Seek ye first the kingdom of God, and his righteousness; and all these things shall be added unto you" (Matthew 6:33; 3 Nephi 13:33). Unlike the wealthy young ruler of Luke 18:18–25, these shepherds were entirely willing to set aside the things of this world for the peace that the angels had offered.

The shepherds found Mary, Joseph, and the Babe not in a house—as the wise men did some time later—but in the cave or pen in which the Son of God had been born.[38]

---•---

LUKE 2:17

And when they had seen it, they made known

> *abroad the saying which was told them concerning this child.*

They made known abroad the saying which was told them concerning this child

The shepherds were among the first mortals to bear witness of the Messiah's advent. After they had seen Jesus, they declared to others what they had been told from a divine source about Jesus. No doubt they confided to Mary and Joseph that they had seen angels. They likely told others in Bethlehem after they left the "manger." The visit of the shepherds would have been important for Mary, as now she knew there were other witnesses to the divine nature of her Child. Mary's relief finds a parallel in the words of the Prophet Joseph after the Three Witnesses had been shown the plates:

> You do not know how happy I am; the Lord has now caused the plates to be shown to three more besides myself. They have seen an angel . . . and they will have to bear witness to the truth of what I have said, for now they know for themselves that I do not go about to deceive the people, and I feel as if I was relieved of a burden which was almost too heavy for me to bear, and it rejoices my soul that I am not any longer to be entirely alone in the world.[39]

Mary too must have felt a sense of relief upon hearing the testimony of the shepherds. As the fourth-century Ambrose of Milan wrote: "An angel tells Mary, an angel tells Joseph, an angel tells the shepherds. It does not suffice that a messenger is sent once. For every word stands with two or three witnesses."[40] All of this left a deep impression upon Mary.

LUKE 2:18–19

*And all they that heard it wondered at those
things which were told them by the shepherds.
But Mary kept all these things, and pondered
them in her heart.*

All they that heard it wondered

Everyone marveled at the miracle of the visit of an angel and the birth of the Messiah and at the testimony of the shepherds regarding these things. The shepherds did not keep silent about the miraculous things they had witnessed. They told whomever they could. As followers of Christ—and bearers of the divine witness that He is the Messiah, the Savior, He who lives—we should follow the example of these foreordained shepherds and lift our voices regarding the greatest miracle of all time—for, like them, we too have marvelous things to declare.

Luke tells us that Mary pondered in her heart the implications of what had happened both to her and to the shepherds. The Greek for "pondered" is literally to "throw side by side" and implies that she thought deeply about what was happening and what she had been divinely called to bring to pass.[41]

Basically, two reactions to the gospel message are illustrated here—the excited shepherds who tell everyone they can, and the pondering Mary who knows that she is in possession of truths that not only escape words but also are likely not appropriately shared with just anyone (compare Matthew 7:6; 3 Nephi 14:6).

———— • ————

JST LUKE 2:20 (KJV LUKE 2:20)

And the shepherds returned, glorifying and praising God for all the things which they had heard and seen, as they were manifested unto them.

And the shepherds returned, glorifying and praising God

The shepherds too were overwhelmed with what the Father had shown them, both in the field and at the manger.

––––––– • –––––––

LUKE 2:21

And when eight days were accomplished for the circumcising of the child, his name was called Jesus, which was so named of the angel before he was conceived in the womb.

The circumcising of the child

For nearly two thousand years all males born into the house of Israel were circumcised at eight days of age (Genesis 17:12). Anciently, the number eight was associated with the concepts of resurrection, new beginnings, rebirth, and baptism. Because of its association with resurrection, the number eight was sometimes also associated with the Messiah.

Circumcision served as a reminder to all Israel of the covenant God had made with Abraham (Genesis 17:11; Acts 7:8). It was a reminder to the parents of the circumcised boy that they were to teach and train their children to obey God's laws in preparation for the day when they would enter into personal covenants with God—when each child reached the age of accountability (JST Genesis 17:11; D&C 68:25). Jesus was no exception.

Upon His circumcision He was given the name

"Yeshua" ("Jesus"), meaning "Jehovah is salvation," for that was the name an angel had commanded both Mary (KJV and JST Luke 1:31) and Joseph (KJV Matthew 1:21; JST Matthew 2:4) to give the child.

LUKE 2:22–24

And when the days of her purification according to the law of Moses were accomplished, they brought him to Jerusalem, to present him to the Lord; (as it is written in the law of the Lord, Every male that openeth the womb shall be called holy to the Lord;) and to offer a sacrifice according to that which is said in the law of the Lord, A pair of turtledoves, or two young pigeons.

They brought him to . . . present him to the Lord

In compliance with the law of Moses, after Jesus was forty days old, Joseph and Mary took Him to the temple, and Mary there offered a sacrifice of purification on her behalf.[42] Upon their arrival at the temple, two separate ceremonies took place. First was the presentation of the child, and then the purification of the mother. Though Luke does not mention it, it is assumed that the usual five shekels were paid to redeem the child, as was required by the law of Moses (Numbers 18:15–16). Joseph Fielding McConkie wrote: "Given that all temple rituals, and for that matter all gospel ordinances, were a type and a shadow that were to testify of Christ, one could only expect that the announcement of his birth must be heard in the temple also. In this anticipation we are not to be disappointed."[43]

———— • ————

JST LUKE 2:25–35 (KJV LUKE 2:25–35)

And behold, there was a man at Jerusalem, whose name was Simeon; and the same man was just and devout, waiting for the consolation of Israel; and the Holy Ghost was upon him. And it was revealed unto him by the Holy Ghost, that he should not see death, before he had seen the Lord's Christ. And he came by the Spirit into the temple; and when the parents brought in the child, even Jesus, to do for him after the custom of the law, then took he him up in his arms, and blessed God, and said, Lord, now lettest thou thy servant depart in peace, according to thy word; for mine eyes have seen thy salvation, which thou hast prepared before the face of all people; a light to lighten the Gentiles, and the glory of thy people Israel. And Joseph, and Mary, marvelled at those things which were spoken of the child. And Simeon blessed them, and said unto Mary, Behold, this child is set for the fall and rising again of many in Israel; and for a sign which shall be spoken against; yea, a spear shall pierce through him to the wounding of thine own soul also; that the thoughts of many hearts may be revealed.

There was a man at Jerusalem, whose name was Simeon

The name Simeon means "God/Yahweh has heard" or "one who hears and obeys." Early legends abound regarding the identity of Simeon. The authenticity of most is uncertain, but the nature of the legends is curious.

- One source says that Simeon was 112 when Jesus was born.

- Another early text claims that Simeon was the father of Rabbi Gamaliel, who years later would wisely advise the Pharisees: "And now I say unto you, Refrain from these men [the apostles of Christ], and let them alone: for if this counsel or this work [Christianity] be of men, it will come to nought: but if it be of God, ye cannot overthrow it; lest haply ye be found even to fight against God" (Acts 5:38–39).

- One texts claims that Simeon was converted to Christianity—not an unlikely suggestion—and that he is the same Simeon mentioned in Acts 15:14.

- Another says of Simeon that he was a high priest in the temple and the successor to Zachariah (John the Baptist's father) in that office.

- Lastly, one legend has it that years after the death of Simeon, Jesus raised his two sons from the dead.

What we know from Luke is that Simeon spoke prophetically about the Christ child. The elderly man was led to the temple that day by the Spirit.[44] He was a righteous man who had been waiting for the "consolation" of Israel (meaning her salvation through the Messiah). In some earlier prophetic utterance, he had been promised that he would not taste of death until he saw the face of the Savior. Now that he had seen the Messiah, he petitioned the Lord to take him. Being moved upon by the Holy Spirit, Simeon spoke of Jesus as the light and salvation of both Israel and the Gentile nations—a concept contrary to the teachings of Judaism in his day.

His words caused Joseph and Mary to marvel, not because they disbelieved but because of how many people God was revealing this concept to and because they were hearing from Simeon's lips more than they had previously known. It was significant and sobering. One commentator reminds us: "There is matter for wonder that Simeon knew all this, and in any case what he says goes far beyond anything the shepherds said. We now find that the whole story is not sweetness and light. Salvation will be purchased at a heavy cost and Simeon soberly records this."[45]

This child is set for the fall and rising again of many in Israel

Through revelation Simeon foresaw that Christ and His gospel message would divide the house of Israel—God's covenant people. As well as saying Jesus would bring the "fall and rising" of Israel, the Greek can also be rendered as meaning that Jesus would bring to pass the "damnation" and the "resurrection" of Israel. Indeed, He would serve as a sign from God that many would reject and thereby become accountable.

A spear shall pierce through him to the wounding of thine own soul

The prophetic Simeon testified that when Jesus was crucified and pierced, Mary's own soul and heart would be pierced. The joy that came to the hearts of Mary and Joseph through Simeon's testimony that Jesus is the Christ was clearly tempered by his additional prophecy of the future suffering and death of God's Only Begotten Son. This might have been Mary's first glimpse into the intense heartache that awaited her. Nevertheless, she was as worthy of God's blessings as a person could hope to be. No doubt she saw God's hand constantly in her life, even in times of overwhelming sorrow.

———— • ————

JST LUKE 2:36–37 (KJV LUKE 2:36–37)

And there was one Anna, a prophetess, the daughter of Phanuel, of the tribe of Asher. She was of a great age, and had lived with a husband only seven years, whom she married in her youth, and she lived a widow of about fourscore and four years, who departed not from

*the temple, but served God with fastings and
prayers, night and day.*

There was one Anna, a prophetess

By "prophetess" is meant one with the gift of
prophecy, rather than the office of a prophet, seer, or revelator. Significantly, Anna is the only woman in the New
Testament to be called a "prophetess."[46] Luke's application
of this title to her highlights her spiritual gifts. She was a
remarkable, spiritually endowed daughter of God.

Anna is said to be of the tribe of Asher and a daughter
of Phanuel. Asher means "fortunate," and Phanuel means
"face of God." It might be conjectured that these names
foreshadowed the blessing Anna would receive in her later
years—seeing the face of the Lord in His infancy.

Luke indicates that, like Simeon, Anna was elderly at
the time of this encounter. We do not know exactly how
old she was, but it does appear that Luke is saying she was
at least 101 years of age.[47]

- In New Testament times women were traditionally
  married at somewhere between twelve and fourteen
  years of age.

- She was married only seven years before the death
  of her husband.

- It had been eighty-four years since her husband died.

- If she had been married at ten years of age, she would be one hundred and one.

- She could easily have been as old as one hundred and five by the time this encounter took place.

According to the Gospel of Luke and various ancient extracanonical texts, Anna departed not from the temple. In so many words, she was a full-time temple worker, which in Christ's day would have consisted mostly of saying prayers and simply lingering at the temple throughout the day.[48]

———— • ————

LUKE 2:38

And she coming in that instant gave thanks likewise unto the Lord, and spake of him to all them that looked for redemption in Jerusalem.

She . . . that instant gave thanks . . . and spake of him to all

Anna's recognition of the Messiah, simply by sight of the infant, was evidence of her prophetic nature. She was receptive to the promptings of the Holy Spirit. One text reminds us:

> Ironically, this singular event was prophesied in ancient times, studied and discussed by scores and scores through the centuries, and yet the occurrence was noted as marvelous by only a handful of Earth's population; they were among the most humble people—shepherds, a carpenter, . . . a widow in the temple, and old Simeon who, before he departed this life, waited for a witness of the Messiah.[49]

Luke informs us that Anna told others who were looking for redemption that she had found the Lord. According to the Greek, she ceased not to speak to others about her testimony that the Messiah had come and that she had seen Him. Thus, we read:

> Luke tells us of but two who held and blessed the Christ child in the temple. Surely there were others—if not within the temple courts, in other places. . . . These would be people ignored by the sacerdotal classes, simple and faithful people who were outside the pale of political rivalry and dispute, people ignorant of the subtleties of Rabbinic argument, people whose personal prayers had reflected

those of Zacharias in their pleadings for the birth of their Messiah.[50]

———— • ————

LUKE 2:39–40

And when they had performed all things according to the law of the Lord, they returned into Galilee, to their own city Nazareth. And the child grew, and waxed strong in spirit, filled with wisdom: and the grace of God was upon him.

And . . . they returned into Galilee, to their own city Nazareth

While at His home Jesus is said to have grown in spirituality and wisdom, because God's grace was upon Him. The Greek says that the "favor of God was upon him." This language is such that it draws our attention back to Luke 2:13–14, where we are told that peace is reserved for those who have the "favor of God" upon them. Even in this, Jesus serves as our Exemplar.

CHAPTER FOUR

THE NATIVITY STORY AS THE GOSPEL IN MINIATURE

A world-renowned biblical scholar once suggested: "The infancy narratives [which tell the story of the birth of Jesus] are worthy vehicles of the Gospel message; indeed, each is the essential Gospel story in miniature."[1] In other words, within the four short chapters of the Gospels of Matthew and Luke, the central message of the gospel of Jesus Christ can be found. As one fascinated by typology, I have pondered this proposition and find both merit and significance in the claim.

Commentators on the fall of Adam and Eve frequently suggest that scriptural descriptions of that great event are intended to describe our personal fall. Thus, we are told, as we read the scriptural accounts, we must liken those accounts to ourselves.[2] Elaine Cannon once observed: "People can be obedient like Mary, be defenders of Christ like Joseph, share the good news like angels, humbly seek the Lord like the shepherds, go to great lengths to bring gifts like the Wise Men. Also, filled with the glowing Spirit of God, they can guide others to Christ like the Star of Bethlehem!"[3]

Thus if the story of the birth of Christ is really the gospel story in miniature, then it appears that we must see ourselves in the story line. We must ask, not simply, How does this story draw me to Christ? but also, How is this story about me and my effort to be what God has called me in this life to be? For example, the announcement in Matthew 1:18 that Jesus' parents were the mortal Mary and the divine Father, even God, is not simply a passing side note. It is the primary point of the Nativity story and a central truth of the gospel plan. Like Christ, we too are of divine origin—sons and daughters of God sent to this earth with a mission. And like Jesus, we have been given earthly parents as guardians and stewards while we are in our youth.

At birth Jesus was wrapped in "swaddling clothes" (Luke 2:7). As previously noted, Luke's emphasis on Christ's being wrapped in these strips may have been to emphasize that this child was born to die. Buried in the story of the Nativity is the key to our salvation: Jesus the Christ was born to die, born to give His life on our behalf.

Jesus was born perfect, innocent, godly, and filled with faith in His Father in Heaven and the great plan of happiness. This aspect of the story reminds all parents that every child is born innocent. Each is sent by God with a mission, much as the Father's Only Begotten in the Flesh had been. And each child of God has the potential to become like the Father, as Jesus has successfully become like the Father. Again, the Nativity's emphasis on the purity and origins of Jesus serves as a reminder of a central tenet of the plan of salvation.

Jesus' mother, Mary, was a virgin, a pure and chosen vessel of God. In the story of the Nativity she exemplifies what God calls *all* mothers to be. Each is given a divine appointment to take care of God's children, whom He will send to earth. Each mother, if she is to be an inspired and successful parent, must be clean and pure, as Mary was. If mothers are to have the gifts of the Spirit requisite to meet the needs of these most precious spirits—those whom they have been assigned by God to nurture and rear—they must be constantly worthy of God's companionship. Elaine Cannon suggested that Mary's comfort came as ours can—only through the power of the Holy Ghost.[4] Mothers must ensure that the Holy Spirit is the source to which they turn for strength and direction, rather than the trappings of this world. Finally, like Mary, mothers must be willing to set aside their will in preference for God's will, even if it requires of them tremendous sacrifice. Again, we read: "While Jesus grew, Mary matured in her own human way, as mothers must. She became a type and shadow for other mothers in every way."[5] God sends children, not simply so that parents can teach them but also so that parents can be taught by these children, just as Mary was taught by Jesus.

Joseph, the earthly guardian and protector of Jesus, was a man who had prophetic visions and dreams. The story of the Nativity, particularly Joseph's example, reminds us of what God has called *all* fathers to be. The humble carpenter was worthy to be the stepfather of the Son of God. Each earthly father is divinely called and appointed to be the mortal parent of one or more of God's spirit children. As Jesus did not *really* belong to Joseph, so children we rear in mortality do not *really* belong to us.[6] They are the children of a loving and protective Father in Heaven, who has assigned us to be the stewards, protectors, and spiritual guides to His offspring. If we fail to honorably and faithfully fulfill that stewardship, serious consequences will be ours. If the fathers of the Church are to save the spiritual lives of God's children, as Joseph saved and protected the physical life of God's Only Begotten Son, they must be visionary, inspired men of God, worthy of the priesthood which they bear.

Joseph and Mary both received the ministry of angels. Mothers and fathers in Zion must also receive the ministry of angels—particularly the Holy Ghost.[7] How else can they expect to succeed as parents? In addition, many of the faithful people spoken of in the story of the Nativity received visitations and heavenly manifestations. The story of the birth of Christ reminds us that as part of the plan of our Father in Heaven, divine communication will be sent to the faithful. These manifestations will not necessarily be in the form of visible angels. Better yet, the promise of the Lord is that they will come in the form of a member of the Godhead—the Holy Spirit. These promptings and manifestations will lead us to Christ (as they did the shepherds) and also safely home (as they did the wise men). To attempt to navigate the pitfalls of mortality (or, for that matter, parenting) without such divine promptings is to commit spiritual suicide.

Herod sought to kill the infant Christ and to destroy the family of Joseph, Mary, and Jesus. Today, evil abounds and seeks to kill the spirituality and well-being of each family of the earth, including the family of God, as found in His Church. Just as Herod posed as one desiring to "worship" the Son of God, so also Lucifer's minions—those who do his bidding—hide their true feelings about the family and the commandments of the Lord. Whether the source of the destruction of the family and Church is governments or social movements, "progressive" religious sects, or concerns for so-called "tolerance," the result is the same: The family, faith in God, and the Church are all under assault. Faithfulness and reliance upon the Divine offered the only protection in Jesus' day; and only that same faithfulness and divine influence will enable us of the latter days to protect our families. In the end, Joseph and Mary were forced to flee to find a safe haven for their family. We too must flee the things of this fallen world if we wish to find a respite from sin, temptation, vice, and spiritual destruction. The story of the Nativity warns us that there is no safety in filling our lives with the things of this world. Rather, safety is to be found in humbly seeking to ever be in tune with the Spirit of the Lord.

God sent the wise men, the shepherds, Simeon, and Anna to testify of Christ. Similarly, God sends each of us multiple witnesses during our mortal probation—all lending their testimony of Christ and His restored gospel. We have the witness of ancient prophets in the Bible, the Book of Mormon, and in the Pearl of Great Price. We have the testimony of the Prophet Joseph Smith and each of his successors. We have inspired bishops and Relief Society presidents. Young Men and Young Women leaders and faithful Primary teachers all testify of Christ and the witness they have received through the Spirit regarding His divine mission and His restored gospel. Thus, as the Nativity story tells us that Mary and Joseph were privileged to receive multiple inspired witnesses of Jesus' divine origins, we too are to expect the same. And like Mary and Joseph, we too can then gain our own personal witness of the truthfulness of this work and of God's plan.

The story of Jesus' birth tells us that the wise men brought gifts of gold, frankincense, and myrrh, traditionally believed to have symbolized the gifts Christ would bring to the world. The gold reminds us that Christ is celestial or godly in His nature. It represents His incorruptibility, purity, and wisdom. It reminds us that He who was sent to redeem us was of royal birth and filled with power. The frankincense symbolizes Christ's sacrifice, constant communion with God, and eventual resurrection. The myrrh was a balm or ointment, highlighting both the suffering of Christ but also His power to atone and to heal. Thus, like the swaddling clothes, in the gifts of the wise men we are reminded of why Jesus came to earth—to suffer, bleed, and die. He was capable of doing so on our behalf specifically because of His godly nature, His purity, and His constant communion with His Father in Heaven.

When Jesus was born, Satan reared his ugly head.

One commentator noted: "The kingdom of God will never go unopposed in the days of the earth's mortality, the period of Satan's power. Evidence of the anger and wrath of hell at the birth of God's Son makes the nativity story complete. The tidings of great joy brought no joy to the prince of darkness or his servants."[8] As it was with Jesus, so it is with each of us. When we strive to do good, we are harassed, tried, and buffeted by the adversary of all righteousness. That is an eternal verity. Light stirs up darkness—and always will. Thus, we must expect opposition to our conscious efforts to live God's laws and keep His commandments.

Certainly much more could be observed. Suffice it to say, truly the Christmas story is the gospel message in miniature. May we read it with the intent of knowing our calling and role in life, keeping God's covenants and commandments, and spreading His gospel, the greatest of all messages.

CHRISTMAS QUIZ: HOW WELL DO YOU KNOW THE STORY OF THE FIRST CHRISTMAS?

As well known as the story of the birth of Christ is, the details are sometimes confused. One commentator wrote:

> No story in the Christian world is more loved than that of the birth of Christ. It is a story to be told and retold. It has been depicted more often in art, heralded more frequently in hymn, spoken of more consistently in churches, and enacted more repeatedly in pageants than any other Bible story. The irony that attends such devotion is the near-universal misunderstanding of the . . . story, not to mention how commonly it is mistold.[1]

Many of us confuse the facts, either combining the details of Matthew's and Luke's accounts or making assumptions that simply are not supported by scripture. In part, we do so because we do not read scripture as carefully as we should. In part, popular culture confuse the story. For example, secular Christmas hymns often teach false doctrine regarding the events surrounding the birth of Christ, and most Christmas Nativity scenes are inaccurate in their depiction of the event.

The following eleven questions represent basic elements of the story that are often misunderstood. Answer each question to the best of your ability and then look at the answers at the end of the quiz. You may be surprised at how many questions you miss. Sources for the answers are in the preceding pages of this book.

Christmas Quiz

1. Jesus was born in a country ruled by what people?

2. What was the relationship between Mary and Elisabeth, the mother of John the Baptist?

3. How did the shepherds find the Christ child?

4. Where did the wise men find Jesus?

5. Other than the wise men, who in the Eastern Hemisphere saw the "new star" that announced the birth of Christ?

6. How many wise men visited the Christ child?

7. Who did Herod order to be killed in Bethlehem?

8. What false notion is taught in the second verse of the Christmas carol "Away in a Manger"?

> *The cattle are lowing, the poor baby wakes;*
> *But little Lord Jesus, no crying he makes.*
> *I love thee, Lord Jesus; look down from the sky*
> *And stay by my cradle till morning is nigh.*
>   (Hymns, *no. 206*)

9. What false notions are taught in the first and second verses of the Christmas carol "It Came upon a Midnight Clear"?

It came upon the midnight clear,
That glorious song of old,
From angels bending near the earth
To touch their harps of gold:
"Peace on the earth, good will to men
From heav'n's all-gracious King."
The world in solemn stillness lay
To hear the angels sing.

Still thru the cloven skies they come
With peaceful wings unfurled,
And still their heav'nly music floats
O'er all the weary world.
Above its sad and lowly plains
They bend on hov'ring wing,
And ever o'er its babel sounds
The blessed angels sing.

(Hymns, *no. 207)*

10. What false notions are taught in the first and second verses of the Christmas carol "With Wondering Awe"?

With wond'ring awe the wise men saw
The star in heaven springing,
And with delight, in peaceful night,
They heard the angels singing:
Hosanna, hosanna, hosanna to his name!

By light of star they traveled far
To seek the lowly manger,
A humble bed wherein was laid
The wondrous little Stranger.
Hosanna, hosanna, hosanna to His name!

(Hymns, *no. 210)*

11. What false notions are taught in the traditional Christmas carol "The First Noel?"

The first Noel the angel did say
Was to certain poor shepherds in fields as they lay,
In fields where they lay keeping their sheep
On a cold winter's night that was so deep.

They looked up and saw a star
Shining in the East beyond them far,
And to the earth it gave great light,
And so it continued both day and night.

(Hymns, *no. 213)*

Other hymnals contain the following additional verses:

And by the light of that same star
Three Wise Men came from country far;
To seek for a king was their intent,
And to follow the star wherever it went.

This star drew nigh to the northwest,
O'er Bethlehem it took its rest;
And there it did both stop and stay,
Right over the place where Jesus lay.

> *Then entered in those Wise Men three,*
> *Full reverently upon the knee,*
> *And offered there, in his presence,*
> *Gold and myrrh and frankincense.*
> (United Methodist Hymnal, *no. 245)*

Answers to the Christmas Quiz

1. The Romans.

2. The King James Version speaks of them as "cousins"; however, the Greek word translated "cousin" does not necessarily mean "cousin" or even "relative." The Greek word can just as readily be translated "neighbor, someone from the same village, someone from the same tribe, or someone with the same political or national affiliations." In other words, the Greek text never calls Elisabeth and Mary cousins, and it is unclear if they were indeed that.

3. They followed the directions of an angel.

4. In his home in Bethlehem.

5. The New Testament implies that no one else saw, or noticed, the star.

6. The scriptures do not say. Because the wise men brought with them three gifts (gold, frankincense, and myrrh), some have assumed that there were three wise men; however, neither the number nor the names of the wise men are given in the scriptures.

7. All children two years or less; that is, all children, male or female, who had not yet reached their third birthday.

8. That Jesus, when a baby, did not cry.

9. That angels play "harps of gold" and have wings.

10. The first error is the claim that the wise men heard the

angels singing. In fact, it was the shepherds who heard the angels speak; the wise men saw the star. The second error is the claim that the wise men sought the manger. In actuality, they sought the home of Christ; the shepherds went to the manger. The wise men arrived much later.

11. First, the hymn inaccurately claims that the birth of Jesus was on a "cold winter's night," perhaps in December. If the shepherds were out "keeping their sheep," it was much more likely spring than winter. Second, contrary to the words of the hymn, the shepherds are not recorded as having seen the star; the wise men saw the star. Indeed, the Bible suggests that the star did not give "great light"; according to Matthew, the star was not universally visible. Third, the hymn claims that there were three wise men; the scriptures are silent about how many there were or what their names were.

APPENDIX 2

MAP OF PALESTINE AT THE TIME OF THE SAVIOR'S BIRTH

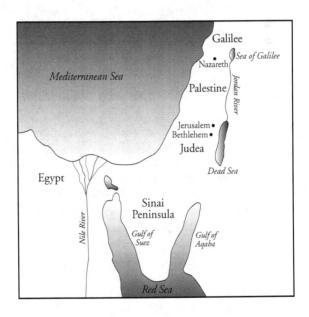

The following lists in chronological order locations of events significant to the Nativity and the early life of Jesus.

1. *Nazareth of Galilee.* The angel Gabriel appeared to Mary

here, informing her of her divine calling to be the mother of the Son of God.

2. *The hills of Judea.* Elisabeth and Zacharias lived here, and Mary spent three months there during the first part of her pregnancy. Although the Bible is silent on exactly what town or village Elisabeth lived in, early Christian tradition suggests that it was a small community known as En Kerim, just west of Jerusalem

3. *Nazareth of Galilee.* Joseph and Mary were living here when the decree of Caesar Augustus was issued regarding the mandatory census and requiring them to travel to Bethlehem, where Jesus was born.

4. *Bethlehem of Judea.* In accordance with the laws of the time and the decree of Caesar Augustus, Joseph and Mary traveled to Bethlehem, where Jesus was born.

5. *Jerusalem.* When Jesus was forty days old, Joseph and Mary traveled to Jerusalem to present him at the temple. There they encountered Simeon and Anna.

6. *Bethlehem of Judea.* Joseph and Mary returned to Bethlehem (after their trip to the temple), and there Jesus spent approximately the first three years of His life. It was also while they were living in Bethlehem that the famous "wise men" made their visit.

7. *Egypt.* During the Holy Family's residence in Bethlehem, Joseph was warned in a dream that he should take his family and flee to Egypt because King Herod desired the death of the Christ child.

8. *Judea.* Upon hearing of King Herod's death (circa 4 B.C.), Joseph returned with his family to Judea. Upon arriving in the region, however, he learned that that Herod's son Archelaus reigned in his father's stead, so Joseph took the family back to Nazareth of Galilee.

9. *Nazareth of Galilee.* From the age of three or four onward Jesus lived in Nazareth. He remained there until He reached adulthood.

WHERE DID MATTHEW AND LUKE LEARN THE STORY OF THE SAVIOR'S BIRTH?

Because neither Matthew nor Luke was present at the birth of Jesus, we know that they were not eyewitnesses to the Nativity. So where did they get their information about Christ's birth? Why do their two accounts differ so greatly in their details?

Before we attempt to answer these questions, it may be helpful to know a bit more about Matthew and Luke.

Matthew and his account

Before his call to the original Quorum of the Twelve Apostles (Matthew 10:1–4), Matthew was a tax collector. In the time of Christ there were two types of tax collectors: those who collected what might be called direct taxes (taxes on individuals and land), and those who collected tolls, or indirect taxes (taxes on goods). The direct taxes were collected by the government, either by the Romans or the tetrarchs. The indirect taxes were exacted by private contractors, who paid the government a flat fee to have the right to collect tolls. Then they would go about collecting as much as they could, because any surplus they collected beyond the amount they contracted with the government for was the collector's profit. One commentator noted: "Such a system lent itself to corruption, dishonesty, and especially to repression of the poor peasantry who attempted to move their produce to market."[1] Thus, the collectors of tolls, or indirect taxes, were considered greedy (Luke 3:12–13) and were usually associated with sinners (Matthew 9:10–11; Mark 2:15; Luke 5:29–30), prostitutes (Matthew 21:31–32; Luke 7:39; 18:11), and Gentiles (Matthew 5:46–47; 18:17). Matthew was one of those who collected tolls, or indirect taxes, although his call to the Twelve certainly implies that he had not succumbed to the corruption for which his profession was notorious.

Of the author of the first Gospel, the LDS Bible Dictionary states: "Matthew was probably a thorough Jew with a wide knowledge of the [Old Testament] scriptures, and able to see in every detail of the Lord's life the fulfillment of prophecy. His Gospel was written for the use of Jewish persons in Palestine, and uses many quotations from the [Old Testament]."[2] Indeed, there are numerous examples of Jewish traditions that Matthew appears to have drawn upon when writing his witness, biblical traditions that Matthew saw Christ's life as fulfilling (compare, for instance, Matthew 2:13–14 and Exodus 2:15; Matthew 2:16 and Exodus 1:22; Matthew 2:19 and Exodus 2:23; Matthew 2:19–20 and Exodus 4:19; Matthew 2:21 and Exodus 4:20).

The date of the composition of Matthew's Gospel is uncertain. Early Patristic evidence has Matthew writing perhaps before the martyrdom of Peter (ca. A.D. 64), or not long thereafter. Contemporary scholars, particularly those who believe that Matthew borrowed much of his material from Mark's Gospel, tend to place the date of the composition of Matthew's Gospel somewhere around A.D. 85 or later. It is impossible at this point to draw any firm conclusion on the matter.

> Of the four Gospels contained in the canon of the New Testament, those of Matthew and John were the most widely read; . . . also, the use of Matthew began far earlier than that of John. Consequently, it is no exaggeration to state that the faithful who lived between the end of the first and the end of the second centuries came to know the words and deeds of Christ on the basis of [Matthew's] text.[3]

Luke and his account

Born to Gentile parents, before his baptism Luke worked as a physician. Some time after his conversion, he served as a missionary companion to the apostle Paul (Philemon 1:24; Colossians 4:14; 2 Timothy 4:11).

Whereas Matthew's Gospel strives to paint a picture of Jesus as the fulfillment of the typological stories of the Old Testament, Luke draws parallels between the lives of Jesus and John the Baptist. For example, both families experience an "annunciation"; both Jesus and John went into the desert; both were foreseen by the prophet Isaiah hundreds of years before their birth; both drew upon the Old Testament for warnings to their followers; both were questioned about their identity; and both preached the Good News of the coming kingdom of God.

Although Luke's Gospel was likely written for Gentile readers, it is uncertain when or where it was composed. As with Matthew's work, commentators vary greatly in their opinions. Dates for the text traditionally range anywhere from A.D. 61 to early in the second century, with most modern commentators placing it around A.D. 80–85.

One commentator wrote: "As one might suspect, [in the ancient church] Luke's Gospel was the obvious choice during the Christmas season because of the unique narratives associated with Jesus' infancy and childhood. This is evident from the Jerusalem lectionary, where Matthew's Gospel is most prominent throughout the year, but Luke takes a prominent place during Christmas."[4] Two thousand years later the Gospel of Luke still seems to hold a position of prominence at Christmastime, including among the Latter-day Saints. One LDS author wrote: "It is to Luke that we owe a debt of gratitude for much of the nostalgia that surrounds Christmas each year. The Gospel of Luke in the New Testament is a treasure in literature not only because of the sacred topic with which it begins but also because of the mood the author creates with the details he includes about the miracle of the birth."[5]

The source for the Nativity stories

One problem with some contemporary scholars' assumption that Matthew and Luke had access to Mark's Gospel when they wrote their own witness of the life of Christ is the absence of the Nativity story in the Gospel of Mark. Mark never mentions Jesus' birth, his youth, or even the name of Jesus' stepfather. If Matthew and Luke did borrow from Mark, they must have had access to other traditions, whether oral or written, that Mark did not have or did not use. Additionally, if Matthew and Luke relied on a single early tradition, we must wonder why their accounts vary so greatly. If they were borrowing from a common source, should not their accounts be at least *almost* identical?

The truth is, we simply don't know where Matthew and Luke received their information regarding Christ's birth. We can only conjecture. However, the most probable options are as follows:

Jesus

It makes complete sense to suggest that Jesus shared the details of His nativity and childhood with His intimate disciples, particularly the Twelve, at some point during His ministry, whether before or after the Resurrection. Once they became members of the Twelve, perhaps Matthew and Luke learned these details from other Apostles who had received these teachings directly from Jesus, or perhaps Jesus appeared to them in a post-resurrection vision. The only puzzlement is that Matthew records some details, whereas Luke records entirely different ones. Perhaps they recorded what struck them the most in the story. Or perhaps they heard the story on separate occasions (from different disciples or in separate visions), and Jesus' emphasis (or the emphasis given by the person who taught them) was different on those occasions.

Mary and Joseph

Because Luke shares Mary's story, and Matthew tells Joseph's account, some have assumed that Luke and Matthew may have obtained their information directly from Jesus' mother and stepfather. That would account for the variation in content between the two Gospels. Mary certainly lived long enough to have shared her story with Luke.[6] But if, as tradition holds, Joseph died before Jesus' ministry, it seems improbable that he could have shared his account of the Nativity with Matthew. Nevertheless, Joseph's possible premature death does not preclude the possibility that he told his story, whether orally or in writing, to someone with whom Matthew later had contact.

It has also been suggested that the differences between the Matthean and Lucan accounts might be attributable to the difference in the audiences to which they addressed their respective narratives. Matthew, of course, was writing to Jews, whereas Luke was writing to Gentiles.

James, the brother of Jesus

James, Jesus' half brother, eventually became an apostle and a member of the early Church's First Presidency.[7] Because of his role as a leader in the early Christian Church and also because he was a member of the family of Jesus, it is likely that at some point Mary, Joseph, Jesus, or perhaps even all three, confided the details of the Nativity to him. If that is so, James could have been the source for Matthew's information, if not for both Matthew's and Luke's accounts.

Oral or written traditions of the early Christians

Some biblical scholars argue that before the writing of the Gospels of Matthew and Luke, oral and perhaps written traditions about Jesus' life and teachings circulated freely among believers. If such sources did exist, Matthew and Luke would surely have been aware of them and could have used any of them as a source for information about the Nativity. "Since it is generally agreed among scholars that Matthew and Luke wrote independently of each other, without knowing the other's work, agreement between the two infancy narratives would suggest the existence of a common infancy tradition earlier than either evangelist's work."[8]

Personal revelation

We know that Matthew was an apostle of the Lord Jesus Christ and as such, a prophet, seer, and revelator. Although Luke's ecclesiastical office is never stated in the Bible, his introduction to his Gospel suggests that he too held that same high and holy calling, and the Prophet Joseph Smith declared that he did.[9] Of his witness and appointment, Luke wrote: "As I am a messenger of Jesus Christ, . . . who from the beginning [was an] eyewitness . . . of the word" (JST Luke 1:1–2). It is hard to rule out as a distinct possibility that Luke and Matthew may have known details of the Nativity by personal revelation. With so many angelic visitations associated with the Nativity story, it seems quite possible—indeed, quite likely—that God might have chosen to reveal the details surrounding the birth of His Only Begotten Son through personal revelation to two spiritually prepared and foreordained witnesses.

In the end, we do not know for certain where Matthew and Luke got their information. Any of the aforementioned sources are possibilities; indeed, a combination of them is possible, too. Significantly, Luke is quite clear that he is not passing along some rumor that had been circulating through the early Church. Rather, he testified to Theophilus: "It seemed good to me also, *having had perfect understanding of all things from the very first,* to write unto thee in order . . . that thou mightest know the certainty of those things" (Luke 1:3–4; emphasis added). His words imply a sound source for his teachings and the receipt of a confirming witness from the Holy Spirit that what he shared regarding the Nativity was historically accurate and divinely sanctioned.[10] The spirit of Matthew's account seems equally sound and divinely inspired.

NOTES

PREFACE

1. In the Doctrine and Covenants the Lord speaks to the Prophet Joseph regarding the Apocrypha, a collection of ancient religious texts held by Latter-day Saints to be extracanonical. Among other things, the Lord says of these nonscriptural religious texts: "There are many things contained therein that are true. . . . Therefore, whoso readeth [them], let him understand, for the Spirit manifesteth truth; and whoso is enlightened by the Spirit shall obtain benefit therefrom" (D&C 91:1, 4–5). It is in the spirit of that inspired counsel that ancient and modern non-LDS texts have sometimes been used in this work.

CHAPTER ONE

1. Bede the Venerable, "Exposition of the Gospel of Luke 2.39," cited in Just, *Luke,* 53.

2. McConkie, *Witnesses of the Birth of Christ,* 10.

3. It should be noted that in many cases the Joseph Smith Translation simply changes the King James Version so that it accords with the original Greek. Thus, many of the Joseph Smith Translation renderings are not corrections to the biblical text but rather improvements on the King James translation, so that it more fully agrees with the original Greek.

4. The Joseph Smith Translation omits the phrase "in thy womb," as it appears in the King James Version.

5. The Joseph Smith Translation omits the phrase "seeing I know not a man," as it appears in the King James Version.

6. The Joseph Smith Translation omits the word "it," as it appears in the King James Version.

7. The Joseph Smith Translation omits the phrase "in the womb," as it appears in the King James Version.

8. The Joseph Smith Translation omits the parentheses around this verse in the King James Version.

9. The Joseph Smith Translation omits the word "thou," as it appears in the King James Version.

10. The Joseph Smith Translation omits the phrase "his mother," as it appears in the King James Version.

11. The Joseph Smith Translation omits the phrase "his mother," as it appears in the King James Version.

12. The Joseph Smith Translation omits the parentheses around the first clause of this verse in the King James Version.

13. Luke's narrative skips from Jesus as a forty-day-old child to Jesus as an approximately three- or four-year-old child; however, a number of significant events in Jesus' life occurred during this time (for example, Herod's desire to kill the Christ child and the resulting "slaughter of the innocents," the visit of the "wise men," the divine warning for Joseph to take the baby and his mother to Egypt, etc.). Matthew covers these significant events, but Luke is entirely silent about them.

CHAPTER TWO

1. Concerning the sources of the details Matthew recorded in his account of the Nativity, see Appendix 3, "Where Did Matthew and Luke Learn the Story of the Savior's Birth?"

2. Ancient genealogies did not traditionally mention women; however, Mary's name is given both in Matthew 1:18 and in Matthew's list of Jesus' full genealogy (Matthew 1:1–17). The presence of Mary's name in the list is a clear indication that something unique or special is going on. In addition, Matthew further breaks with tradition by listing the names of five women in Jesus' genealogy: Tamar, Rahab, Ruth, Bathsheba (Uriah's wife), and Mary. Although we cannot be certain why their names are listed, biblical commentators suggest that the presence of women in the list emphasizes the role of providence or divine intervention. The presence of these specific women in Jesus' lineage may be intended to show that despite their

less than ideal history, God still intervened through them to ensure the accomplishment of His plan and to preserve the line of the Messiah. Each of the women clearly played an important role in bringing to pass God's plan and thus must be considered an instrument in God's hands. Because Mary's pregnancy would certainly have been looked upon as scandalous by most in her day, the acknowledgment that God preserved the Davidic/Messianic line through other women with "scandalous backgrounds"—women accepted in covenant Israel as instruments in the hands of God—could negate criticism of Mary and the virgin birth. One early Christian text rightly notes that Jesus "was appropriately born contrary to the law of human nature because he was beyond nature. Behold the strange and wonderful birth of Christ. It came through a line that included sinners, adulterers and Gentiles. But such a birth does not soil the honor of Christ. Rather, it commends his mercy" ("Incomplete Work on Matthew, Homily 1," in Simonetti, *Matthew,* 13).

3. McConkie, *Mortal Messiah,* 1:317; see also Talmage, *Jesus the Christ,* 83–84.

4. Brown, *Birth of the Messiah,* 123–24.

5. See Talmage, *Jesus the Christ,* 84. On the other hand, Joseph Fielding McConkie implies that Joseph knew that Mary was pregnant before she left for her extended stay at Elisabeth's home. According to Brother McConkie, it was after Mary left for Elisabeth's that Joseph had his vision informing him that the baby was of God: "Following this dream he immediately sent for Mary, asking her to take her rightful place at his side. . . . Thus the Christ child was born in wedlock" (*Witnesses of the Birth of Christ,* 35). The chronology is unclear, not only because ancient witnesses speak of Joseph's dismay at seeing Mary's size some time after her return from Elisabeth's, but more particularly because in most ancient versions of Luke he speaks of Joseph and Mary as still "espoused" (rather than married) when Mary gave birth to the Christ child (Luke 2:4–5). Matthew seems to imply that Joseph married Mary but then had no intimate relations with her until after Jesus' birth (Matthew 1:24–25). I am of the opinion that Joseph's angelic vision telling him that Mary's pregnancy was of God came at a time *after* Mary's return from Elisabeth's, when Mary would have begun to become "great with child" (Luke 2:5) and thus able to be "found out" or "discovered" (as the Greek of Matthew 1:18 implies she

was). Admittedly, when Mary first returned from Elisabeth's home, her physical state would not necessarily have indicated pregnancy, particularly in light of the flowing robes customarily worn at the time. However, the text is unclear how soon after Mary's return Joseph "discovered" she was pregnant. It may have been several months, or perhaps it was through Joseph's vision of the angel. We simply have no way of knowing.

Similarly, we have no record regarding when the wedding of Joseph and Mary took place. Matthew and Luke simply do not appear to agree on the matter. Some commentators hold that Mary and Joseph were still *not* officially or fully married at the time of Jesus' birth but, rather, were still in the state of espousal. Others argue that Mary and Joseph were married before Jesus' birth. Some have even gone so far as to suggest that Mary and Joseph had already married before the birth but were called "betrothed" because the marriage had not yet been consummated—which is the primary distinction between "fully married" and "betrothed." In support of this last claim, it should be noted that a few ancient versions of Luke speak of Mary not as Joseph's "betrothed" but as "his wife."

6. "The Protevangelium of James," v. 13, in Roberts and Donaldson, *Ante-Nicene Fathers,* 8:364; see also "The Gospel of Pseudo-Matthew," chap. 10, in Roberts and Donaldson, *Ante-Nicene Fathers,* 8:373. Another reading of the events is found in Elder Bruce R. McConkie's *Messiah* series, in which he conjectures: "We may well suppose that Mary told Joseph of her condition; that she *then* went to Elisabeth; that Joseph struggled with his problem for nearly three months, being fully tested; that [an angel] brought the word; that Joseph sent word to Mary of his conversion; that she returned again in haste and joy; that immediately the second part of the marriage ceremony was performed; and that Joseph, to preserve the virginity of the one who bore God's Child, refrained from sexual association with her until after Jesus came forth as her child" (*Mortal Messiah,* 1:333; emphasis added). Others conjecture differently. Joseph Fielding McConkie writes that Matthew says Mary "'was found with child.' This suggests that she did not volunteer information relative to her state but rather let it be discovered. Nor should it be supposed that Mary told Joseph that she carried the 'child of the Holy Ghost.' The nature of the conception of the child was made known to Joseph by the angel in a dream. He did not learn it from Mary" (*Witnesses of the Birth of Christ,* 32).

7. See, for example, Brown, *Birth of the Messiah,* 124; Robinson, *Nag Hammadi Library,* 143.

8. Many Latter-day Saints have traditionally understood that God fathered the Child and that the Holy Spirit's presence was necessary for Mary to endure the glory of God without being destroyed (see Pratt, *The Seer,* 158–59). Although many more could be given, the following sources define both what is meant by Jesus being "the Only Begotten of the Father in the Flesh" and also the procreation of Jesus, the latter being something we simply cannot fully understand: Joseph F. Smith, cited in Brewster, *Doctrine and Covenants Encyclopedia,* 398–99; Rodney Turner, in Peterson and Tate, *Pearl of Great Price,* 93; Brigham Young, in *Journal of Discourses,* 4:218; 11:122, 268; McConkie, *New Witness for the Articles of Faith,* 67; Heber C. Kimball, in *Journal of Discourses,* 6:101. The position of The Church of Jesus Christ of Latter-day Saints about the parentage of Jesus Christ is expressed in 1 Nephi 11:18–21.

9. See Robert L. Millet, "The Birth and Childhood of the Messiah," in Jackson and Millet, *Studies in Scripture,* 5:142.

10. In Clark, *Messages of the First Presidency,* 4:329. As to how the conception of Jesus took place, the late fourth-century Christian father John Chrysostom wisely counseled: "Do not speculate beyond the text. Do not require of it something more than what it simply says. Do not ask, 'But precisely how was it that the Spirit accomplished this in a virgin?' . . . Shame on those who attempt to pry into this miracle . . . from on high! For this birth can by no means be explained, yet it has witnesses beyond number. . . . Neither Gabriel nor Matthew has explained, nor is it possible" (Chrysostom, in Simonetti, *Matthew,* 12–13). Similarly, one LDS author wrote, "The details of this miracle are delicately veiled in the holy scriptures" (Cannon, *Christmas Crèche,* 8).

11. Admittedly, because of the size of the community in which Mary lived, there was no way to keep this scandal hidden, nor any way to shield her from the consequent embarrassment, but Joseph did what he could to make all of this as private and nonhumiliating as possible.

12. Chrysostom, "The Gospel of Matthew, Homily 4.4," in Simonetti, *Matthew,* 14.

13. This is not to say that the Jewish authorities of Joseph and Mary's day would have enforced the death penalty for adultery. We simply do not

know if such was the case. However, the law of Moses is quite clear on the issue.

14. See McConkie, *Mortal Messiah,* 1:316. Cyril of Alexandria wrote: "The divine law commanded that marriages should be confined to those of the same tribe" ("Commentary on Luke, Homily 1," in Just, *Luke,* 38).

15. Because Joseph is not mentioned after Jesus' twelfth year, a false tradition has arisen that he was *much* older than Mary—being at least 91 when Jesus was born. This theory suggests that Joseph had been married before his betrothal to Mary and was a widower with six children. According to the legend, he hesitantly took Mary as his wife and was only willing to do so because the Lord revealed that such was His will. The Bible makes no such claims regarding Joseph. Individuals bent on calling Mary a "perpetual virgin"—refusing to believe that she and Joseph had children after the birth of Jesus—have created a story to explain away both the brothers and sisters of Jesus (Matthew 13:55; Mark 6:3) and also the supposed premature death of Joseph. The Bible never states that Joseph was dead by the time Jesus began His mortal ministry; however, the lack of mention of Joseph at that point suggests that such was likely the case. Nevertheless, the idea that Joseph was 111 years old when he died—and this several years before Jesus announced His Messiahship—goes well beyond what the text would allow. If Joseph was indeed dead by the time Jesus began His ministry, it seems as reasonable to assume that he died of some disease, accident, or of natural causes (in his forties) as it does to conjecture some wild story about Joseph being a twice-married man of 111. True, the culture of the day traditionally had the husband as the older of the two marital partners; however, a seventy-five- to eighty-year span between Joseph and Mary simply is not likely, culturally or otherwise.

16. Matthew speaks of Joseph as Mary's "husband" and of Mary as Joseph's "wife," whereas Luke uses neither term without connecting them with the phrases "betrothed" or "espoused," in all probability to avoid any misunderstanding about who Jesus' true Father was.

17. Elder Bruce R. McConkie wrote: "As with all men, his faith and his willingness to submit to the divine will in all things must be tested" (*Mortal Messiah,* 1:331).

18. In Millet and Jackson, *Studies in Scripture,* 5:144.

19. As to the identity of the "angel of the Lord," see the usage of the

term in the Hebrew of Genesis 16:7, 13; 22:11, 14; Exodus 3:2, 4; Judges 6:12, 14; Hosea 12:4; Isaiah 63:9. See also Brown, *Birth of the Messiah,* 129; Meyers and Myers, *Haggai, Zechariah 1–8,* 180, 183; Carol A. Newsom, "Angels," in Freedman, *Anchor Bible Dictionary,* 1:250; Kidner, *Genesis,* 33, 127.

20. As one commentator put it, Joseph likely "spent a restless night after he learned about Mary's being pregnant before their marriage" (Cannon, *Christmas Crèche,* 22).

21. Chromatius, "Tractate on Matthew, 2:3–4" in Simonetti, *Matthew,* 15.

22. McConkie, *Mortal Messiah,* 1:332–33.

23. Until about the beginning of the second century after Christ, the name Jesus was very common among Jews; from then onward, however, it disappeared as a proper name (see Kittel and Friedrich, *Theological Dictionary of the New Testament,* 3:285–86; Walter L. Liefeld, "Luke," in Gaebelein, *Expositor's Bible Commentary,* 8:831). For Matthew, "his people" meant both Jews and Gentiles—all of the children of God (see Brown, *Birth of the Messiah,* 130–31).

24. See McConkie, *Witnesses of the Birth of Christ,* 25; Brown, *Birth of the Messiah,* 166–67; Albright and Mann, *Matthew,* 12; McConkie, *Mortal Messiah,* 1:349–50, n. 2; Clark, *Our Lord of the Gospels,* 168–74; Edersheim, *Life and Times of Jesus the Messiah,* 164. Regarding the implications of Doctrine and Covenants 20:1 on the question of when Jesus was born, see Woodford, "Historical Development of the Doctrine and Covenants," 1:286–301; Grant Underwood, in Ludlow, *Encyclopedia of Mormonism,* 1:410; Smith and Sjodahl, *Doctrine and Covenants Commentary,* 138; Richard Lloyd Anderson, "The Organization Revelations," in Millet and Jackson, *Studies in Scripture,* 1:113–15.

25. See Appendix 2, "Map of Palestine at the Time of the Savior's Birth."

26. The Catholic religious holiday known as Epiphany is a commemoration of the visitation of the wise men to the Christ child. Epiphany is celebrated on January 6 rather than December 25, specifically because the biblical text makes it clear that Jesus had long since left the manger before the wise men arrived bearing gifts. Of course, The Church of Jesus Christ of Latter-day Saints accepts neither December 25 as the

date of Christ's birth nor January 6 as the date of the arrival of the wise men. These dates were selected by fourth-century Christians to supplant pagan celebrations. Nevertheless, if Jesus was born in April, and the wise men arrived in January, then Jesus would have been somewhere between nine months and two and three-fourths years of age when they arrived.

27. Joseph Fielding McConkie notes that like so many others in this great story, the wise men too would have been foreordained to their call in the councils of heaven before the creation of this earth (*Witnesses of the Birth of Christ,* 94).

28. McConkie, *Doctrinal New Testament Commentary,* 1:103.

29. McConkie, *Mortal Messiah,* 1:358.

30. Elder James E. Talmage offers Numbers 24:17 ("there shall come a star out of Jacob, and a Scepter shall rise out of Israel") as a possible prophetic text from which the wise men may have been working (*Jesus the Christ,* 99). Joseph Fielding McConkie notes: "Though this prophecy is frequently associated with the story of the wise men it is not without significance that Matthew, who constantly provides us with proof-texts—some of which are rather forced—makes no reference to it" (*Witnesses of the Birth of Christ,* 98; see also commentary on KJV Matthew 2:4 and JST Matthew 3:4).

31. Note that Alma does not say that Jesus would be born "in" Jerusalem; rather, he says Christ would be born "at" Jerusalem, meaning "near," "by," or in the region "surrounding."

32. Although technically the "city of David" is Jerusalem (not Bethlehem), nevertheless, Luke uses the phrase "City of David" in reference to Bethlehem (Luke 2:4; 2 Samuel 5:7, 9; David Tarler and Jane M. Cahill, "David, City of," in Freedman, *Anchor Bible Dictionary,* 2:53; Fitzmyer, *Gospel According to Luke,* 406). Brown notes that Bethlehem was the city of David's origin, to which he returned for family occasions, but that Jerusalem (not Bethlehem) would have the distinction of being the "City of David" (*Birth of the Messiah,* 396; see also Appendix 2, "Map of Palestine at the Time of the Savior's Birth").

33. Josephus indicates that the title of "king of the Jews" had been officially given to Herod, in all likelihood because of "contributions" Herod had made to Caesar (see Josephus, *Antiquities of the Jews,* 14.4, in Whiston, *Complete Works of Josephus,* 308).

34. In Millet and Jackson, *Studies in Scripture,* 5:149.

35. Joseph Fielding McConkie wisely noted: "Whereas *some* among the faithful in the Old World were aware of a new star announcing the night of his birth, in the New World 'at the going down of the sun there was no darkness,' and throughout all the land *all* saw the star announcing his birth. (See 3 Nephi 1:14–17.)" (*Witnesses of the Birth of Christ,* 4; emphasis added).

36. McConkie, *Witnesses of the Birth of Christ,* 97.

37. "The Protevangelium of James," v. 21, in Roberts and Donaldson, *Ante-Nicene Fathers,* 8:366; emphasis added. This ancient document is attributed to James, the son of Mary and Joseph and thus Jesus' half brother.

38. Again, if the star was universally visible, it seems only logical that Herod would have had his men follow it (as the wise men did) straight to the residence of Mary and Joseph.

39. As noted above, it is puzzling that most simply did not see or recognize this star. The Book of Mormon also speaks of it but uses language that, again, could have very dualistic intentions. It notes that at the Lord's birth there were "great lights in heaven" (Helaman 14:3)—notice that "lights" is plural. The book of Helaman states that "there shall a new star arise, such an one as ye never have beheld; and this also shall be a sign unto you" (Helaman 14:5). Such a statement does not preclude John or Abraham's use of the term "star" as a symbol for an angel or for the Son of God. Certainly Christ was "new" and "as one" they had "never beheld." The statement in 3 Nephi 1:21, that "a new star did appear, according to the word," also leaves open the possibility of a dualistic interpretation.

40. After all, Mary and Joseph both received angels regarding the matter—and the shepherds abiding in the fields were visited by an angel who instructed them how to find the baby Jesus. It seems strange that these wise men would be treated so differently. Why the text would call an angel a "star" only when speaking of the wise men is unclear.

41. See "The Gospel of Pseudo-Matthew," chapter 17, in Roberts and Donaldson, *Ante-Nicene Fathers,* 8:376.

42. For texts that compare the lives of Moses and Christ, see Gaskill, *Lost Language of Symbolism,* 185–88; Grant and Tracy, *Short History of the Interpretation of the Bible,* 34; McConkie, *New Witness for the Articles of Faith,* 154–57.

43. Chrysostom, "The Gospel of Matthew, Homily 8.2," in Simonetti, *Matthew,* 31.

44. McConkie, *Mortal Messiah,* 1:366, n. 1. See also McConkie, *Witnesses of the Birth of Christ,* 105.

45. Millet and Newell, *Jesus, the Very Thought of Thee,* 16. For more on the possible number of children killed, see McConkie, *Mortal Messiah,* 1:362–63.

46. Cannon, *Mary's Child,* xiii.

47. Brown, *Birth of the Messiah,* 206. See also France, *Gospel According to Matthew,* 87.

48. See Appendix 2, "Map of Palestine at the Time of the Savior's Birth."

49. Jerome explained: "If this could have been found in the Scriptures, he never would have said, 'Because it has been spoken by the prophets,' but he would rather have spoken more plainly: 'Because it has been spoken by *a* prophet.' As it is now, in speaking of prophets in general he has shown that he has not taken the specific words but rather the sense from the Scriptures. 'Nazarene' is understood as 'holy.' Every Scripture attests that the Lord was to be holy. We can also speak in another way of what was written . . . in Hebrew in Isaiah: 'A branch will blossom from the root of Jesse, a Nazarene from his root'" (Jerome, "Commentary on Matthew, Book 1, 2:23," in Simonetti, *Matthew,* 37). Another commentator noted: "The name of Nazarene was but another word for *despised one.* Hence, although no prophet has ever said anything of the word Nazarene, yet all those prophecies describing the Messiah as a *despised one* are fulfilled in his being a Nazarene" (*Unger's Bible Dictionary,* 779).

50. Clark, "Wist Ye Not That I Must Be about My Father's Business?" *Relief Society Magazine,* February 1944, 78; or McConkie, *Mortal Messiah,* 1:374.

51. McConkie, *Mortal Messiah,* 1:163.

52. Smith, *History of the Church,* 6:50.

CHAPTER THREE

1. Regarding where Luke may have acquired the details found in his account of the Nativity, see Appendix 3, "Where Did Matthew and Luke Learn the Story of the Savior's Birth?"

2. It is curious that Gabriel makes the declaration to Mary that she is highly favored of God, as it was said of him some twenty-four hundred years earlier: "Noah was *highly favored* of the Lord" (Genesis 6:8, LXX Translation).

3. McConkie, *Mortal Messiah,* 1:23.

4. See McConkie, *Mortal Messiah,* 1:326–27, n. 4.

5. Walter L. Liefeld, "Luke," in Gaebelein, *Expositor's Bible Commentary,* 8:830–31. See also Morris, *Luke,* 80.

6. Church, *NIV Matthew Henry Commentary,* NT 214.

7. Joseph Fielding McConkie conjectured: "If Joseph alone had been descended from David, Mary should have answered, 'I am not yet married to Joseph,' but instead she simply answered 'I am an unmarried woman,' which implies that if she were married her son would have right by birth to David's throne. The difficulty was not one of descent but that Mary knew not a man" (*Witnesses of the Birth of Christ,* 63).

8. Smith, *History of the Church,* 4:540.

9. Ambrose, "Exposition of the Gospel of Luke, 2:14," in Just, *Luke,* 18.

10. See Kittel and Friedrich, *Theological Dictionary of the New Testament,* 7:740–41; Thayer, *Greek-English Lexicon of the New Testament,* 592, s.v. no. 4773; Brown, *Death of the Messiah,* 2:292; Ben Witherington III, "Elisabeth," in Freedman, *Anchor Bible Dictionary,* 2:474; Vine, *Expository Dictionary of New Testament Words,* 250, s.v. "Cousin"; Strong, *Concise Dictionary of the Words in the Greek Testament,* 67, s.v. no. 4773.

11. McConkie, *Mortal Messiah,* 1:319.

12. Morris, *Luke,* 82.

13. McConkie, *Mortal Messiah,* 1:319–20.

14. Cannon, *Mary's Child,* 3.

15. Maximus of Turin, "Sermon 5:4," in Just, *Luke,* 21. See also Church, *NIV Matthew Henry Commentary,* NT 215.

16. Browning, *Gospel According to Saint Luke,* 41.

17. Walter L. Liefeld, "Luke," in Gaebelein, *Expositor's Bible Commentary,* 8:834.

18. This passage contradicts the idea of the Immaculate Conception, which holds that from the moment of her conception, Mary was (by God's grace) "kept free from all taint of Original Sin." In this passage

Mary acknowledges her need for a Savior and thus, being mortal, must have committed sin (see Walter L. Liefeld, "Luke," in Gaebelein, *Expositor's Bible Commentary,* 8:836; see also Church, *NIV Matthew Henry Commentary,* NT 215; Morris, *Luke,* 84).

19. Origen, "Homilies on the Gospel of Luke, 8:1–3," in Just, *Luke,* 24–25.

20. McConkie, *Witnesses of the Birth of Christ,* 67–68.

21. Bede the Venerable, "Homilies on the Gospels, 1.4," in Just, *Luke,* 25.

22. Morris, *Luke,* 85. See also Walter L. Liefeld, "Luke," in Gaebelein, *Expositor's Bible Commentary,* 8:836.

23. Brown, *Birth of the Messiah,* 337.

24. Augustine, "Sermon 290.6," in Just, *Luke,* 26.

25. The Greek word translated in the King James Version as "taxed" most likely should be translated "census" (see Thayer, *Greek-English Lexicon of the New Testament,* 60; Brown, *Birth of the Messiah,* 394; Nicoll, *Expositor's Greek Testament,* 1:470). Joseph Fielding McConkie wrote: "It was not the payment of taxes that brought Joseph and Mary from Nazareth to Bethlehem. Nor did Caesar Augustus have the power to tax 'all the world.' His authority to tax rested only with the Roman Empire. What was required by Caesar Augustus was a census. Had Judea been, as she would yet become, a mere Roman province, her census would have been taken after the Roman method; since she was still a kingdom, it was taken after the Jewish method, which required each person to repair to his ancestral seat to be recorded. It could hardly be supposed that the Jewish system would require one in Mary's delicate state to travel from Nazareth to Bethlehem. Mary and Joseph came from Nazareth to Bethlehem because they knew that in the providence of heaven the Christ child was to be born in Bethlehem, which was the original family home for them both" (*Witnesses of the Birth of Christ,* 70; see also Brown, *Birth of the Messiah,* 391–96).

26. Whereas Matthew speaks of Joseph as Mary's "husband" and of Mary as Joseph's "wife" (Matthew 1:19–20), Luke uses neither term without connecting it with the phrases "betrothed" or "espoused," in all probability to avoid any misunderstanding about who Jesus' true Father was. See Brown, *Birth of the Messiah,* 125.

27. Walter L. Liefeld, "Luke," in Gaebelein, *Expositor's Bible Commentary,* 8:844.

28. "The Arabic Gospel of the Infancy of the Saviour," v. 4, in Roberts and Donaldson, *Ante-Nicene Fathers,* 8:405.

29. Gregory Thaumaturgus, "The First Homily: On the Annunciation to the Holy Virgin Mary" and "The Second Homily: On the Annunciation to the Holy Virgin Mary," in Roberts and Donaldson, *Ante-Nicene Fathers,* 6:60, 65.

30. Church, *NIV Matthew Henry Commentary,* NT 218. Many commentators have assumed that "swaddling clothes" were the common covering of most newborns of the era; however, the acclaimed biblical scholar Joseph Fitzmyer questions this assumption. He asks why, if swaddling clothes were so common, was that a sign to the shepherds who would seek out the child? (see Fitzmyer, *Gospel According to Luke,* 410).

31. Cirlot, *Dictionary of Symbols,* 183.

32. Ambrose, "Exposition of the Gospel of Luke 2.41–42," cited in Just, *Luke,* 38.

33. McConkie, *Witnesses of the Birth of Christ,* 71.

34. Lefgren, *April Sixth,* 15–16. "Concerning the date of Christ's birth, one of the earliest known references to December 25 was in the third century A.D. Scholarly consensus recognizes that early Christians probably appropriated December 25 from pagan festivals. . . . Presidents of the Church, including Harold B. Lee . . . and Spencer W. Kimball . . . have reaffirmed that April 6 is the true anniversary of Christ's birth, but have encouraged Church members to join with other Christians in observing Christmas as a special day for remembering Jesus' birth and teachings" (John Franklin Hall, "April 6," in Ludlow, *Encyclopedia of Mormonism,* 1:61–62).

35. McConkie, *Witnesses of the Birth of Christ,* 74.

36. Beers, *Victor Handbook of Bible Knowledge,* 325, as cited in McConkie, *Witnesses of the Birth of Christ,* 80.

37. McConkie, *Mortal Messiah,* 1:347. Joseph Fielding McConkie conjectured that these very shepherds to whom the angel appeared had been foreordained "in the councils of heaven to be the first earthly witnesses of the birth of Christ" (*Witnesses of the Birth of Christ,* 78).

38. The shepherds arrived on the night of Christ's birth. The wise men arrived much later, whether weeks, months, or years is unclear.

39. Smith, *History of the Church,* 1:56, footnotes.

40. Ambrose, "Exposition of the Gospel of Luke 2.51," cited in Just, *Luke,* 40. See also Deuteronomy 17:6; 19:15; Matthew 18:16; 2 Corinthians 13:1; 1 Timothy 5:19; Hebrews 10:28; D&C 6:28; 128:3.

41. Bede the Venerable wrote: "Mary wished to divulge to no one the secret things which she knew about Christ. . . . However, though her mouth was silent, in her careful, watchful heart she weighed these secret things" ("Homilies on the Gospels 1.7," cited in Just, *Luke,* 43). Bede goes on to say that Mary was well aware of the many messianic scriptures that were being fulfilled in her very own life, and she likely reviewed these one by one, all the while in awe at her part in this.

42. "The Levitical law provided that after the birth of a son a woman would be unclean for seven days and that for a further thirty-three days she should keep away from all holy things (Leviticus 12:1–5). Then she should offer a lamb and a dove or pigeon. If she was too poor for a lamb a second dove or pigeon sufficed instead (Leviticus 12:6–13). Mary's offering was thus that of the poor" (Morris, *Luke,* 96–97).

43. McConkie, *Witnesses of the Birth of Christ,* 83.

44. Luke 2:25–27 makes it clear that the Holy Ghost was operative before the Day of Pentecost (see LDS Bible Dictionary, s.v., "Holy Ghost," 704).

45. Morris, *Luke,* 98.

46. Ben Witherington III, "Anna," in Freedman, *Anchor Bible Dictionary,* 1:257. Some five different women in the Old Testament bear the title of prophetess: Miriam, the sister of Moses (Exodus 15:20); Deborah (Judges 4:4); Huldah (2 Kings 22:14; 2 Chronicles 34:22); Noadiah (Nehemiah 6:14); and Isaiah's wife (Isaiah 8:3).

47. Millet and Jackson, *Studies in Scripture,* 5:148. Although commentators traditionally understand the passage to be saying that Anna's husband had been dead some 84 years, there is textual support for the variant reading that she was an eighty-four-year-old woman who was also a widow (see Brown, *Birth of the Messiah,* 442; Morris, *Luke,* 99; Walter L. Liefeld, "Luke," in Gaebelein, *Expositor's Bible Commentary,* 8:851, n. 37; Fitzmyer,

Gospel According to Luke, 431; McConkie, *Witnesses of the Birth of Christ,* 91). There is no way to know for certain which reading Luke intended.

48. Cannon, *Mary's Child,* xii-xiii.

49. McConkie, *Witnesses of the Birth of Christ,* 92.

CHAPTER FOUR

1. Brown, *Birth of the Messiah,* 7.

2. See, for example, Gaskill, *Savior and the Serpent;* Neusner, *Enchantments of Judaism,* 53–65; Bloesch, *Essentials of Evangelical Theology,* 1:103–9.

3. Cannon, *Christmas Crèche,* 26.

4. Cannon, *Mary's Child,* 71.

5. Cannon, *Mary's Child,* 4.

6. This should *not* be taken to imply that families are somehow anything less than eternal; however, God is the Father of the eternal part of each of us. Our earthly parents simply create our physical bodies—which, although used throughout our mortal probation, will eventually become bodies eternal. Thus, even though relationships developed here (or in the premortal world) will continue beyond the veil, in the end, God is our *true* Father—our Eternal Father.

7. See Oaks, "The Aaronic Priesthood and the Sacrament," 38–39.

8. McConkie, *Witnesses of the Birth of Christ,* 115.

APPENDIX 1

1. McConkie, *Witnesses of the Birth of Christ,* vii.

APPENDIX 3

1. Dennis C. Duling, "Matthew," in Freedman, *Anchor Bible Dictionary,* 4:621.

2. LDS Bible Dictionary, s.v. "Matthew," 729.

3. Simonetti, *Matthew,* xxxvii. See also D. A. Carson, "Matthew," in Gaebelein, *Expositor's Bible Commentary,* 8:19.

4. Simonetti, *Matthew,* xix.

5. Cannon, *Mary's Child,* 7.

6. Early Christian tradition supports the notion that Mary shared

her experiences—including that of the Nativity—with Jesus' apostles and disciples: "Bartholomew . . . said to Peter, Andrew, & John, 'Let us ask [Mary] the favored one how she conceived the Lord and bore him.' . . . After much hesitation [Bartholomew] approaches Mary on behalf of the other apostles, and she agrees to enlighten them" (*The Gospel of Bartholomew,* as cited in Nibley, *Mormonism and Early Christianity,* 49).

7. James, the son of Mary and Joseph, replaced James of Zebedee (upon his martyrdom) as first counselor in the First Presidency of the Church (see C. Wilfred Griggs, in Ludlow, *Encyclopedia of Mormonism,* 2:758). Hugh Nibley conjectures that James was also the first Presiding Bishop of the Church in the meridian of times (see *Mormonism and Early Christianity,* 31–36).

8. Brown, *Birth of the Messiah,* 34. Although overall the two accounts seem quite different, there are numerous parallels. Both Matthew and Luke speak of Mary and Joseph as espoused; both note Jesus' Davidic descent; both record an angelic announcement of Jesus' birth; both record the angelic command that the infant should be named Jesus; both speak of the role of the Holy Ghost in the conception of Jesus; both mention that the angel announced that Jesus would be the Savior; both state that the birth took place at Bethlehem; both indicate that the birth of Jesus took place in the days of Herod the Great; and both indicate that Jesus was reared in Nazareth.

9. *Times and Seasons* 3, 21 (1 September 1842): 902.

10. Joseph Fielding McConkie wrote: "This is not a story concocted after the fact to give support to a nativity tradition and thus one written by someone knowledgeable in the detail of the law. It is one written in the naiveté of a Gentile who in all likelihood had no real understanding of the importance of Christ's complying with these rituals, their symbolic importance, or the manner in which they testify of his divine sonship" (*Witnesses of the Birth of Christ,* 93).

SOURCES

In an effort to keep this small volume reasonably accessible, I have limited the number of notes as well as direct quotations from other authors. Information in this text was drawn from study of many sources, including the following:

Achtemeier, Paul J., ed. *Harper's Bible Dictionary.* San Francisco, Calif.: Harper San Francisco, 1985.

Adamson, James B. *The Epistle of James.* A volume in *The New International Commentary on the New Testament* series. Grand Rapids, Mich.: Eerdmans, 1976.

Albright, William F., and C. S. Mann. *Matthew.* Vol. 26 of *The Anchor Bible* series. New York: Doubleday, 1971.

Baldwin, Joyce G. *Haggai, Zechariah, Malachi.* A volume in *Tyndale Old Testament Commentaries.* Downers Grove, Ill.: InterVarsity Press, 1972.

Baring-Gould, S. *Legends of the Patriarchs and Prophets and Other Old Testament Characters from Various Sources.* New York: American Book Exchange, 1881.

Beers, V. Gilbert. *The Victor Handbook of Bible Knowledge.* Wheaton, Ill.: Victor Books, 1981.

Benson, Ezra Taft. *Come unto Christ.* Salt Lake City: Deseret Book, 1983.

Bloesch, Donald G. *Essentials of Evangelical Theology.* 2 vols. Peabody, Mass.: Hendrickson Publishers, 2001.

Brewster, Hoyt W., Jr. *Doctrine and Covenants Encyclopedia.* Salt Lake City: Bookcraft, 1988.

Brown, Raymond E. *The Birth of the Messiah.* Rev. ed. New York: Doubleday, 1993:

———. *The Death of the Messiah.* 2 vols. New York: Doubleday, 1994.

Browning, W. R. F. *The Gospel According to Saint Luke.* Rev. ed. London: SCM Press Ltd., 1979.

Bullinger, E. W. *Number in Scripture: Its Supernatural Design and Spiritual Significance.* Grand Rapids, Mich.: Kregel Publications, 1967.

Cannon, Elaine. *Mary's Child.* Salt Lake City: Bookcraft, 1997.

———. *The Christmas Crèche.* Salt Lake City: Bookcraft, 1998.

Church, Leslie F., ed. *The NIV Matthew Henry Commentary in One Volume.* Grand Rapids, Mich.: Zondervan, 1992.

Cirlot, J. E. *A Dictionary of Symbols.* 2d ed. New York: Philosophical Library, 1971.

Clark, James R., comp. *Messages of the First Presidency of The Church of Jesus Christ of Latter-day Saints.* 6 vols. Salt Lake City: Bookcraft, 1965–75.

Clark, J. Reuben, Jr. *Our Lord of the Gospels.* Salt Lake City: Deseret Book, 1974.

———. "Wist Ye Not That I Must Be about My Father's Business?" *Relief Society Magazine,* February 1944, 78.

Clarke, Adam. *Clarke's Commentary.* 6 vols. New York: Methodist Book Concern, n.d.

Conner, Kevin J. *Interpreting the Symbols and Types.* Portland, Oreg.: City Bible Publishing, 1992.

Cooper, J. C. *An Illustrated Encyclopaedia of Traditional Symbols.* London: Thames and Hudson, 1995.

Cornwall, Judson, and Stelman Smith. *The Exhaustive Dictionary of Bible Names.* New Jersey: Bridge-Logos Publishers, 1998.

Cruse, C. F., trans. *Eusebius' Ecclesiastical History.* Rev. ed. Peabody, Mass.: Hendrickson Publishers, 1998.

Danker, Frederick W. *Luke.* A volume in *Proclamation Commentaries* series. Philadelphia: Fortress Press, 1976.

Davis, John J. *Biblical Numerology.* Grand Rapids, Mich.: Baker Book House, 2000.

Dummelow, J. R. *A Commentary on the Holy Bible.* New York: Macmillan, 1936.

Edersheim, Alfred. *The Life and Times of Jesus the Messiah.* Grand Rapids, Mich.: Associated Publishers and Authors, n.d.

———. *Sketches of Jewish Social Life.* Peabody, Mass.: Hendrickson Publishers, 1994.

Ehat, Andrew F., and Lyndon W. Cook, eds. *The Words of Joseph Smith: The Contemporary Accounts of the Nauvoo Discourses of the Prophet Joseph.* Provo, Utah: Religious Studies Center, Brigham Young University, 1980.

Farrar, Frederic W. *The Life of Christ.* Portland, Oreg.: Fountain Publications, 1964.

First Presidency. "The Father and The Son: A Doctrinal Exposition by the First Presidency and the Twelve." *Improvement Era,* August 1916, 935.

Fitzmyer, Joseph A. *The Gospel According to Luke, I-IX.* Vol. 28 of *The Anchor Bible* series. New York: Doubleday, 1970.

Fontana, David. *The Secret Language of Symbolism.* San Francisco, Calif.: Chronicle Books, 1994.

France, R. T. *The Gospel According to Matthew.* A volume in *Tyndale New Testament Commentaries* series. Grand Rapids, Mich.: Eerdmans, 1997.

Freedman, David Noel, ed. *The Anchor Bible Dictionary.* 6 vols. New York: Doubleday, 1992.

Gaebelein, Frank E., ed. *The Expositor's Bible Commentary.* 12 vols. Grand Rapids, Mich.: Zondervan, 1976–92.

Gaskill, Alonzo L. *The Lost Language of Symbolism: An Essential Guide for Recognizing and Interpreting the Symbols of the Gospel.* Salt Lake City: Deseret Book, 2003.

———. *The Savior and the Serpent: Unlocking the Doctrine of the Fall.* Salt Lake City: Deseret Book, 2005.

Ginzberg, Louis. *The Legends of the Jews.* 7 vols. Philadelphia: Jewish Publication Society of America, 1967–69.

Grant, Robert, and David Tracy. *A Short History of the Interpretation of the Bible.* 2d ed. Philadelphia: Fortress Press, 1984.

Griggs, C. Wilfred. *Apocryphal Writings and the Latter-day Saints.* Provo, Utah: BYU Religious Studies Center, 1986.

Hartin, Patrick John Christopher. "James: A New Testament Wisdom Writing and Its Relationship to Q." Th.D. diss., University of South Africa, 1988.

Hymns of The Church of Jesus Christ of Latter-day Saints. Salt Lake City: The Church of Jesus Christ of Latter-day Saints, 1985.

Ieron, Julie-Allyson. *Names of Women of the Bible.* Chicago: Moody Press, 1998.

Johnson, Luke Timothy. *Sacra Pagina: The Gospel of Luke.* Collegeville, Minn.: Liturgical Press, 1991.

Johnston, Robert D. *Numbers in the Bible: God's Design in Biblical Numerology.* Grand Rapids, Mich.: Kregel Publications, 1990.

Journal of Discourses. 26 vols. Liverpool: Latter-day Saint's Book Depot, 1854–86.

Julien, Nadia. *The Mammoth Dictionary of Symbols.* New York: Carroll and Graf, 1996.

Just, Arthur A., Jr., ed. *Luke.* Vol. 3 of *Ancient Christian Commentary on Scripture,* edited by Thomas C. Oden. Downers Grove, Ill.: InterVarsity Press, 2003.

Kidner, Derek. *Genesis.* A volume in *Tyndale Old Testament Commentaries* series. Downers Grove, Ill.: InterVarsity Press, 1967.

Kittel, Gerhard, and Gerhard Friedrich, eds. *Theological Dictionary of the New Testament.* 10 vols. Grand Rapids, Mich.: Eerdmans, 1984.

Ledbetter, Curtis E. "The Shepherd's Flock." *Ensign,* April 1973, 6–12.

Lefgren, John C. *April Sixth.* Salt Lake City: Deseret Book, 1980.

The Lost Books of the Bible. New York: Bell Publishing, 1979.

Ludlow, Daniel H., ed. *Encyclopedia of Mormonism.* 4 vols. New York: Macmillan, 1992.

McBrien, Richard P., ed. *The Harper Collins Encyclopedia of Catholicism.* San Francisco: Harper San Francisco, 1995.

McConkie, Bruce R. *Doctrinal New Testament Commentary.* 3 vols. Salt Lake City: Bookcraft, 1987–88.

———. "Eve and the Fall." In *Woman.* Salt Lake City: Deseret Book, 1979.

———. *The Millennial Messiah.* Salt Lake City: Deseret Book, 1982.

———. *The Mortal Messiah.* 4 vols. Salt Lake City: Deseret Book, 1980–81.

———. *A New Witness for the Articles of Faith.* Salt Lake City: Deseret Book, 1985.

McConkie, Joseph Fielding. *Gospel Symbolism.* Salt Lake City: Bookcraft, 1985.

———. *Witnesses of the Birth of Christ.* Salt Lake City: Bookcraft, 1998.

McConkie, Joseph Fielding, and Donald W. Parry. *A Guide to Scriptural Symbols.* Salt Lake City: Bookcraft, 1990.

Machen, John Gresham. *The Virgin Birth of Christ.* New York: Harper and Row, 1930.

Meyers, Carol L., and Eric M. Myers. *Haggai, Zechariah 1–8.* A volume in *The Anchor Bible* series. New York: Doubleday, 1987.

Millet, Robert L., and Lloyd D. Newell. *Jesus, the Very Thought of Thee:*

Daily Reflections on the New Testament. Salt Lake City: Deseret Book, 2002.

Morris, Leon. *Luke.* A volume in *Tyndale New Testament Commentaries* series. Rev. ed. Grand Rapids, Mich.: Eerdmans, 1999.

Myers, Allen C., ed. *The Eerdmans Bible Dictionary.* Grand Rapids, Mich.: Eerdmans, 1987.

Neusner, Jacob. *The Enchantments of Judaism: Rites of Transformation from Birth through Death.* Atlanta: Scholars Press, 1991.

Nibley, Hugh. *Mormonism and Early Christianity.* Vol. 4 of *The Collected Works of Hugh Nibley.* Salt Lake City and Provo, Utah: Deseret Book and FARMS, 1987.

———. *Apostles and Bishops in Early Christianity.* Salt Lake City and Provo, Utah: Deseret Book and FARMS, 2005.

Nicoll, W. Robertson, ed. *The Expositor's Greek Testament.* 5 vols. Grand Rapids, Mich.: Eerdmans, 1983.

Nolland, John. *Luke 1–9:20.* Vol. 35A of *Word Biblical Commentary.* Dallas, Texas: Word Books, 1989.

Oaks, Dallin H. "The Aaronic Priesthood and the Sacrament." *Ensign,* November 1998, 38–39.

Parry, Donald W., Jay A. Parry, and Tina M. Peterson. *Understanding Isaiah.* Salt Lake City: Deseret Book, 1998.

Peloubet, F. N. *Peloubet's Bible Dictionary.* Holt, Rinehart, and Winston: New York, 1947.

Peterson, H. Donl, and Charles D. Tate, Jr., eds. *The Pearl of Great Price: Revelations from God.* Provo, Utah: BYU Religious Studies Center, 1989.

Pratt, Orson. *The Seer.* Reprint, Salt Lake City: Eugene Wagner, 1963.

Rest, Friedrich. *Our Christian Symbols.* New York: Pilgrims Press, 1987.

Reynolds, George, and Janne M. Sjodahl. *Commentary on the Book of Mormon.* 7 vols. Salt Lake City: Deseret Book, 1955–61.

Sources

Roberts, Alexander, and James Donaldson, eds. *The Ante-Nicene Fathers.* 10 vols. Peabody, Mass.: Hendrickson Publishers, 1994.

Roberts, B. H. *The Seventy's Course in Theology, Second Year.* Salt Lake City: Skelton Publishing, 1908.

Robinson, James M., ed. *The Nag Hammadi Library.* Rev. ed. San Francisco, Calif.: Harper San Francisco, 1988.

Ryken, Leland. *Dictionary of Biblical Imagery.* Downers Grove, Ill.: InterVarsity Press, 1998.

Simonetti, Manlio. *Matthew.* Vol. 1A of *Ancient Christian Commentary on Scripture,* edited by Thomas C. Oden. Downers Grove, Ill.: InterVarsity Press, 2001.

Smith, Hyrum M., and Janne M. Sjodahl. *Doctrine and Covenants Commentary.* Salt Lake City, Utah: Deseret News Press, 1932.

Smith, Joseph. *History of The Church of Jesus Christ of Latter-day Saints.* Ed. B. H. Roberts. 2d ed. rev. 7 vols. Salt Lake City: The Church of Jesus Christ of Latter-day Saints, 1932–51.

———. *Teachings of the Prophet Joseph Smith.* Sel. Joseph Fielding Smith. Salt Lake City: Deseret Book, 1976.

Smith, Joseph Fielding. *Church History and Modern Revelation.* 2d series. Salt Lake City: The Council of the Twelve Apostles, 1948.

Smith, William. *A Dictionary of the Bible.* Chicago: John C. Winston Company, 1884.

Speiser, E. A. *Genesis.* A volume in *The Anchor Bible* series. New York: Doubleday, 1962.

Strong, James. *A Concise Dictionary of the Words in the Greek Testament.* Nashville, Tenn.: Thomas Nelson Publishers, 1990.

Studies in Scripture. Edited by Kent P. Jackson and Robert L. Millet. 8 vols. Salt Lake City: Deseret Book, 1986–93.

Stuhlmueller, Carroll. *Rebuilding with Hope: A Commentary on the Books of Haggai and Zechariah.* Grand Rapids, Mich.: Eerdmans, 1988.

Talmage, James E. *The Articles of Faith.* Salt Lake City: The Church of Jesus Christ of Latter-day Saints, 1975.

———. *Jesus the Christ.* Salt Lake City: The Church of Jesus Christ of Latter-day Saints, 1981.

Thayer, Joseph H. *Thayer's Greek-English Lexicon of the New Testament.* Peabody, Mass.: Hendrickson Publishers, 1999.

Todeschi, Kevin J. *The Encyclopedia of Symbolism.* New York: Berkley Publishing Group, 1995.

Tresidder, Jack. *Symbols and Their Meanings.* London: Duncan Baird Publishers, 2000.

The United Methodist Hymnal. Nashville, Tenn.: United Methodist Unger Publishing House, 1989.

Vine, W. E. *An Expository Dictionary of New Testament Words.* Westwood, N.J.: Fleming H. Revell, 1966.

Wigram, George V. *The Englishman's Greek Concordance of the New Testament.* Peabody, Mass,: Hendrickson Publishers, 1998.

Wilson, Walter L. *A Dictionary of Bible Types.* Peabody, Mass.: Hendrickson Publishers, 1999.

Whiston, William, trans. *The Complete Works of Josephus.* Grand Rapids, Mich.: Kregel Publications, 1981.

Woodford, Robert J. "The Historical Development of the Doctrine and Covenants." Ph.D. diss., Brigham Young University, 1974.

Young, Edward J. *The Book of Isaiah.* 3 vols. Grand Rapids, Mich.: Eerdmans, 1997.

INDEX